'Sometimes I'm the China Shop....'

A poetry collection:

By Leon the poet

EARTH ISLAND BOOKS

Published by Earth Island Books
Pickforde Lodge
Pickforde Lane
Ticehurst
East Sussex
TN5 7BN

www.earthislandbooks.com

Copyright remains with the authors
First published by Earth Island Books 2024
Cover art by @jacksonbollocksart

No part of this publication may be reproduced, distributed or transmitted by any means, electronic, mechanical, photocopying, or otherwise without written permission from the author.

ISBN 9781916864467

Printed and bound by Solopress, Southend

With thanks to James Domestic, my good friend Luke for all his encouragement, for Loredana for calling me an 'Artist'.

For my Mum who taught me how to work hard, and for my Dad who taught me how to listen.

Most importantly this book is for my kids, Lexi, and Alex, and for 10-year-old me, who never believed.

Contents

1) Soft Play Tales — 1
2) I do love the old guy — 4
3) A lethal dose of hope — 5
4) First Aid — 9
5) Ticking all the boxes on the best of bonkers bullshit to believe in — 13

6) The hollowed-out tree and the cherry red leaf — 17
7) It's just war — 20
8) Everything is invented — 24
9) Madness — 29
10) There are so many things that I'll never be — 34

11) FYI — 37
12) The flower — 43
13) A joker just like me — 45
14) Eulogy for the living — 49
15) The Tories on tour — 51

16) A fleeting moment of honesty — 53
17) 2 things my dog hates. Pigeons and Postman — 54
18) Small boats vs the Tories live on sky sports — 57
19) I wanna be mine — 61
20) Lifestyle choice — 63

21)	Fuck them	67
22)	Open secrets, invertebrates, and fundamentalist Christians	70
23)	A shrug is a silent shove	75
24)	The Elephant	78
25)	Daily hate mail: A public service announcement	84
26)	Games I play with my family at Christmas	87
27)	A new name	88
28)	The best years of your life	90
29)	Cancer for tea	95
30)	The cool kid	96
31)	The Cult Kid and me	99
32)	Parker pens	104
33)	The Artists Manifesto	107
34)	What to say?	110
35)	Death by orange	112
36)	Friends take time	115
37)	The worst gig in the history of the world	117
38)	You're still one of us	125
39)	Ollie and Marie	127

40)	The flying fist, the smile, and the eye	131
41)	A bit of dignity please	136
42)	God is dead	140
43)	The artist/narcissist	143
44)	400 metre champion	145
45)	Hope is all we have, it's all we need	147
46)	Do you ever feel like you've been cheated?	151
47)	Make it happen	153
48)	A list of things I did today	159
49)	My god Harry Styles is boring	160
50)	My Puppy wants to die	162
51)	The homeless girl	165
52)	Man flu	170
53)	Pound shop Moses and the mechanical Red Sea	173
54)	Dear bro	175
55)	A depressed Monday	180
56)	Jimmy is not a meme	182
57)	20 years too late	185
58)	An Amnesty	190
59)	Kurt Cobain's myth making nearly gets me punched square in the kisser	196
60)	A hug from the moon	198

61) Life is absurd, people are ridiculous, and
    nothing matters   200
62) My kid could paint that   207
63) Big cheese   208
64) #Trainwanker   210
65) Who will get custody of all the good times?   213

66) Ash   216
67) Dear person in front of me   218
68) Written, directed by and starring me   221
69) Subway was invented by a man who hated
    people who loved sandwiches   225
70) An arm in cast, a brain in a jar, a liver
    in vinegar   228

71) Man tries to discuss the enlightenment
    with a sausage dog   229
72) Good boy   232
73) My Blue haired Clementine   236
74) Mr Velcro can't let it go   239
75) A pragmatic decision to hate you   242

76) Bernie: The musical   245
77) If God was good and kind   247
78) You can't be properly parented by
    a bureaucracy   250
79) The Room   252
80) Dry Wells   254

81) Under the bridge downtown with Anthony Kiedis and Alicia Keys	256
82) The cold war kiss	261
83) Frank Turner has a lot to answer for	262
84) The Diary of a psycho CEO	266
85) Smudge	269
86) Kill me now	272
87) Hit them where it hurts	273
88) AA but for people addicted to business	274
89) Calling in sick to my boss	280
90) Depressed with the potential for cabaret and violence	281

My kids have long since passed the age of soft plays, but I still find them fascinating. Sit and people watch and you will find all the wonder and minutiae of life. Make sure you bring a kid though.

Soft play tales

In between the shrieks, the coughs, and the laughter
And the low rumble of a baby's cry
Tiny feet pad the floor

Mums whoop in exaggerated praise
Or over explain
'Right, we are going to have a 5-minute break in a minute because you're getting a bit tired, and you didn't sleep too well last night, did you? and you're just getting over a cold'

While her saucer eyed toddler just stares

The dads encourage their boys to find the highest slide and throw themselves down it
They feel a strange flush of pride
If they get to the bottom and don't cry
All bones
All fingers and toes
Happily, Intact
'Not 1 single tear love, he's a proper lad!'

A dad struts into the soft play like it's a saloon bar
A bowler with a stroller
A zero-skin fade back and sides

The kind of dad who likes to play at drowning his kids
Machismo spread so thick
Big foot would get stuck in it

He plays at punching the punch bags and barking at his boy
The kind of love that was built to destroy
Or maybe it's just my PTSD
Seeing threats where there aren't any

This is the under 5's area so it's all very quiet and civilised
The biggest controversy is a kid climbing up the slide
His middle-class dad panics and gives him a good-natured dressing down
But loud, so everyone else watching can hear it
He's asked to leave, and he's outraged
'*But we read the guardian* 'he explains
It cuts no dice
So, he scoops up young Cassidy
Who has been caught bang to rights

'It's because he's got a cold
He's been up all night'
No, it's because he's a little shit
And that's alright that's fine
He's only 5

In the older kids bit
It's much more of a 'Lord Of The Flies' vibe
I can feel every sparkle in my eye extinguish and die

Natural birth control
Soft play tickets should be in the chemists next to the Condoms and the morning after pills
The shouting and the carnage and the bloodshed is pure sensory overload
An apocalyptic war zone
Mad Max with balls pits, climbing nets and jugs of blackcurrant cordial weak as piss

At closing time
The cleaners come in and just hose it all down
Turn off the lights
Start again tomorrow
More babies, more bodies
More mums and dads

But not Cassidy

He's banned.

My dad features quite a lot in this book, but in the midst of all the poems and the endless figuring out of him, remember this ....

I do love the old guy

My first memories of him
Lying on his side
Whistling the siren
He must have done something right

His hair now mostly white
His optimism is endless
Delusional I guess
He keeps going though

I love his vulnerability
His creativity
His boundless positivity
However misplaced it may be

He shouldn't feel guilty
He never was a failure
to me

This is a call and response poem, read this out loud and get the audience to shout

'YES WE CAN'

A Lethal dose of hope

A lethal dose of hope
The kind that hits you in the throat and makes you choke
It plugs all the holes in all the boats
Keeps those migrants afloat
Wins all the votes
100 million Volts

Remember when Obama said
'Yes, we can!'
The question he was answering was
Can we keep things exactly the same?
*'Erm yeah
Yeah, we can'*

I'm asking now
Can we ever make real change?

Can we, do it?
Yes, we can

Can we do it
Yes, we can

Hope has been corporatised

Whitewashed and sanitised
A meme an advert
A fridge magnet
A greeting card
A movement

A brand

'There's a lot of money in that hope brand
That's a good racket right now my man
The wellness industry is booming
Get some shares
Invest in crypto though
Cos' the banks are going down bro'

Can we, do it?
Yes, we can
Can we, do it?
Yes, we can

Hope
Hits you like an endorphin rush
Like all adverts must
Leaves us flushed and flush

It's buy or bust
In the market we trust
Like Liz Truss
The one who royally fucked us

12 years of austerity and they are still
Doing this shit to us

Reducing the deficit
How can you talk of the big society
When 1% have got all the fucking money?

Can we, do it?
Yes, we can
Can we, do it?
Yes, we can

Hope leaves us with some foolhardy sense
That we can still make a difference
In the face of all the facts to the contrary
It lifts us high up on its shoulders and says *come follow me*

Real hope cannot be monetised
It's the one thing that keeps us alive
The wellness industry is booming
You know what else is booming?

Suicide

Self-harm

Social media you sell us the illness and then you sell us the cure
I thought that was what religion was for

We need a lethal dose of hope
To counter the killer dose of despair
Since Covid fixed it
Took the globe and spun it

It's been apocalyptic
Not at all cryptic
Despair
Death and decay

You had better make way
For the end of the world, they say

Hope is not naive
It's more than belief
It's so much more than belief
It's based on evidence

All you've been through
If we pooled all our collective human suffering
We could find the elixir
The holy grail
The antidote

The hope that can keep us from going under
Keep us afloat

Can we, do it?
Yes, we can

Can we, do it?
Yes, we can

First, there was Aiden.

'First Aid'.

Once he was a babe in arms loveable and calm
The apple of his young parent's eyes
Dad just turned 25
Life stretching out before his eyes
Him and his young bride

The dad is now 65, his son as helpless as a child
Once again, a babe in arms but not nearly so loveable and calm

His decline has been undramatic but no less palpable
Hollywood glamourises the mentally unwell
Give them something skilful and interesting to temper the obvious human suffering

A prodigy
A genius
Assigning meaning to the meaningless
And we act all surprised at the lies

The conditioning goes deep friends
All the way to a molecular level
It's in our DNA to believe this is how the hopeless travel
A by-product of genius, the madness
The sadness less keen because of what they can glean from it

A sonnet
A story
A paean to former glories
The reality is far more brutal and banal

For him no grand unravelling, or unveiling
Just a flickering candlelight choking and fading
The chip chip away at his sense of self
The chip chip away at his mental health

Once he had a job and a car
Girls he would call and meet up with and friends at the bar
He was aloof and arrogant and took pride in himself

He was a figure of fun to us because that's what we do
We joke and take the piss
Humour the blackest hue

We were mean at times but that all stopped as we saw the road his life took
His decline

No grand unravelling, no dramatic flourish
Just year upon year upon year of decay
Say what you will, blame who you may
A house abandoned to the elements, absent tenants
Windows and doors boarded
There was however some forewarning

It cannot be fixed now father it's done
The stone has been thrown long ago

All you can do is watch the ripples

Creating chaos with the pain, unresolved anger the same
The horse has bolted 30 years ago, the door is sagging off its frame

The horse is now ten types of dog food, it's insane!
Dad it is far too late.

I'm from a family of runaways
Run away to the army
To England
To God
He'll save us from thinking ever of anything more than what's above

Detached always at a distance, nothing can be fully loved and known at such a grasp
Being held out
At arm's reach
He fell at last

No surprises any more for him it's done
All that's left to do is run
The voices are tormenting him now
The whispers have become
Too loud to bear
He wants to run from there, but to where?

Back to 83, the last place he was truly happy
At 7 years old things made sense totally

A small village school
A family

No god
No meaning
No meetings
No deceiving
No odd nagging at the bones
No guilt feelings

The stone was thrown then by you
When you were searching for some meaning
Something big to aspire to
There is a God, and he loves me
Not only that he has chosen me
He has chosen me

The arrogance is the stone thrown by your father
The abandoned home
The broken wishbone
The fairy tale
The noose
The time for action came far too late
Chasing the stones you've thrown
Across the lake as it undulates

Don't chase father, just wait.

Just wait.

I saw these guys at rush hour by the side of the road. Usually activism is the preserve of the young, so it was refreshing to see these older guys getting involved. Although they gave their age away with their lack of desire to do this more than once, hence why they hit all the major issues in one night.

Ticking all the boxes on the best of bonkers bullshit to believe in

By the side of the road
Yellow placards are held
Middle aged white guys in high vis jackets
Ticking all the boxes on the best of bonkers bullshit to believe in

They start strong by claiming that *'climate change is wrong'*
Poor old BP
That benevolent purveyor of energy
Like Willy Wonka or Walt Disney

Never did a thing to harm anybody
Will no one stand up for the corporate little man
That last year earned 23 billion pounds

Let's link hands
Let's get some daisy chains from man to man for poor old BP getting destroyed by the woke police

Next, they go for Covid with *'don't vax kids'*
Russell brand would be beaming with pride at this

'Unvaxxed and still alive states one placard'

Oooo your hard

I don't blame anyone for this collective amnesia
Someone took this world and shook it like a snow globe
All the conspiracies from the darkest corners of the internet, came showering down upon us like the Ash of Pompeii

David Icke was back in vogue all of a sudden
Everyone conveniently forgetting he once claimed to be the son of God
'Yeah, but that was ages ago'
Didn't he think the queen was a lizard?
'Yeah, but he makes some good points though'

'Lockdowns don't work' they go on to say
Well, it was a global pandemic
So, it's understandable some mistakes were made
And some money was made

Where some see disaster
Others see dollar signs

Where some see dollar signs
They also find
Corruption
Conjecture
Conspiracy

And somehow it always ends up being the fault of……

the Jews

Finally, they finish off with a real classic
The 'Brown Sugar', 'My Generation', 'Hey Jude' of conspiracies

The ultimate boogie man

Immigration!

'No more illegals we are full'

There's so much shit written about this subject
It's impossible to separate the rhetoric from the reality
But let's boil it down to something simple
And catchy
Something that could sit neat on a placard
How about

'Desperate families on boats are not your enemy'

Or

'You are stooges for the ruling classes
They sit back fat and smugly rub their hands while you doff your cap and wipe their arses'

How's that for multi taskers?

I can't parse this
Move past this
There's nothing left to do but sit back struck dumb

aghast at this
Farcical shit
What year exactly did the whole world lose it?

Honk if you believe the placards say

There was precious little honks I'm pleased to say
And for that tiny fact I am thankful at least

Thankful for tender mercies

And the sweet release
Of death

A surreal and dreamlike argument with my dad that happened when we visited a memory from 1988.

The hollowed-out tree and the cherry red leaf

We meet my parents for a walk at Danbury lakes
This place might aswell be a memory we made
There's the hollowed out fallen tree I fell through aged 3
There's where we took that picture of me

The ground is squashy from too much rain
Soft dew nestles bubbling on butterscotch leaves
We squelch down the crooked path and round

We speak in hushed but happy sounds

The leaves have started to curl and turn
Mustard yellow and cherry red
We stomp airily through piles of them

We pass the still and steady lake
We all look out across the water
The sunlight shimmers, glimmers, and shakes
4 ducks wobble by in a perfect V

Dads behind us, connected only by a thread
A baby's breath
Like a kite over head

On the wind we can hear the echoes of childhood laughter
This is our never ever after

I pass us all as children
Posing for pictures

Mums in her knee-high boots
Hair long and straight
Dads smile from his eyes spreads out to his face

This nostalgia feels like the bitterest kind of bliss

We pass the ice cream van
We buy 99s with a flake just cos' we can

We've nearly made it to the car

We've nearly made it

Dad gets out his lighter and starts to flick it
He speaks of a distant cousin unknown to me until this moment
Late teens early 20s
Wasting his life
Retrained as a long-distance lorry driver
Sounds like a future serial killer

And then the kicker

'You know the thing about your little brother is, whenever he sets his mind to something he does it '

The lake starts to ripple
A dull sob from that hollow tree
There is blood on the dewy autumn leaves

As the world screams
And knocks dad clean off his feet

Just or not, all war is the same. It's Armageddon from the skies. We count the cost, but they pay the price.

It's just war

The just war is righteous and right
The just war is the star-spangled banner rippling with all its might
The just war makes us so damn proud to be wherever we are from

The just war has magic bullets and smart bombs
It has missiles that see children and magically pivot around them
It drops aid to the innocent and fire to the enemy

The just war sets up schools and brings democracy
The just war has soldiers greeted with white hankies and ticker tape
In the just war there is no rape

The just war leaves hospitals and schools and sanitation and the fabric of a sovereign nation
Entirely intact

Like a magician pulling endless rabbits from hats!
Ta da!
The just war is noble
Has valour and values
The just war is just
Cos it's us
And we are the good guys

Right?
That's us

Fighting to keep peace and restoring order to the world
Just a bobby on the beat
On civvy street

Giving Iraq a clip round the ear, and Libya a stern look and telling Afghanistan he better run home now and stop playing football in the street

Ah the bobby on the beat
The good ole days
The just wars of the past when everything made sense
When there were goodies and baddies, and PTSD didn't exist
And Guantanamo bay
Reminded us only of the Cuban missile crisis
And not internment
Torture
State sponsored murder

The unjust war is a different kind of beast
The unjust war has refugees who we can welcome into our families
Open the doors
What's mine is now yours
Take the food out of my mouth of course
Take the shirt right off my back
Marry my daughter
I've written you into my will

I'll take you out to dinner and always foot the bill

The unjust war has relief concerts and charity drives
The unjust war has pictures and names of everyone that dies
The unjust war has no regard for the sanctity of life
it steals little kids from their parents' beds at night
The unjust war is so cruel
The unjust war is littered with war crimes
Kids used as human shields that's not alright
We should use our 'just war' weapons
The ones that deploy in seconds
The ones that reduce the world to dust in seconds
Nuclear Armageddon beckons
The last thing anyone on this earth will do, will be to post a meme or a snarky tweet or 2

The just wars
Are never just of course
The weapons don't discriminate
They just obliterate

All war is hell is such a cliche
But it should say 'all war is money' because it sure does pay

Sadly, there's not as much money to be made in peace
No big bumper paydays for the super fucking elite
Add murder to the never-ending rap sheet

It's just business

This business will be the end of us
We need some super-human will to stave off the end of us

Calm down mate

it's just war

Yep, even dogs.

Everything is invented

If you ever feel intimidated
Or self-conscious
Or overcome with the weight of your own head on your shoulders
Or your voice cracks into a high squeak
Or you can't find the right words when you speak
Or you forget how to respond to a simple question
Or you feel like an alien masquerading as a human

Or you get panicked at talking to a policeman
Or a teacher treats you like shit every time he meets ya

Or you feel like an outcast and a misfit
All the time
Cos you don't have your ducks all lined up right
You're not the right shape
With the right face
Or neurotype

Or you feel like you're too sensitive to live this life
And you'll burst into flames if you get held up to the light

Or your doctor makes you feel foolish for calling up about a splatter of freckles that have turned oddly yellow
Or you get caught in the low flying sneer of a

vacuously beautiful fellow

Or your friends are earning big bucks
Sucking corporate cocks
Holidaying in Dubai
On 50 metre yachts

And you're slumming it big time
With the have nots
While they have
And have and have
The whole lot

While their brushing their teeth with foie gras
In gold lined fur coats
Incapable of taking a joke
They only smile to show their glossy new teeth
And open their mouths to blow smoke

If you ever feel small
Feel the weight of the world
Tugging the skin off your cold bones
And fear taking hold

Just remember ....

Everything is invented

Schools
GCSEs
Masters
Degrees
PhDs

1sts, 2.1's
2.2's

Here's the news

It's all invented

Distinctions
universities

Job applications
And CVS

Doctors
Nurses
Every kind of job in fact

It's all invented

Acting
Singing
Walking up and down in a straight line and pouting

Every type of sport
Kicking a lump of leather around for a quarter of a million pound

It's all invented

Why is the news the same on every channel in every paper
All of it culled from the state
Like communist Russia

Propaganda from Pravda

It's all invented

All the different types of
Salesman
Some come to your door
Selling soap
Or hope
Or god
Or both

It's all invented

Politics

I don't subscribe to left or right
I don't dig a trench in this culture war and fight
It's all a distraction
Conspiracies
Are an invention
Older than the wheel
Sponging benefit claimants goes back to the poor
law of 1834

It's all invented

Antisemitism goes all the way back to the bible
The big man himself
Telling his people their special
But if you screw up, I just might kill you

It's all invented

This is not an excuse for nihilism
It's a port in the storm
A rock to steady yourself on

Everything is invented

Even you
Your thoughts and your story made you
Tell yourself something new

And be invented over again

Like everything

My older brother loved his music and used to go and buy records from a really young age. We grew up listening to our parents old Vinyl records, so I guess he just absorbed that love of music too. He would go out and buy madness records and the beach boys. I loved music too but not as much as him. I loved him more than I loved music. I was more desperate for him to like me. So when the time came for me to buy my first 7 inch single, I chose a song that I knew he would like. And that song was 'Diamond Lights' by Glenn Hoddle and Chris Waddle. That's how much I loved him. I bought that piece of shit.

Madness

My brother's favourite band when we were kids was Madness
The bittersweet irony not lost on me
He grew up to be a Schizophrenic you see
Lost in a fog of psychotropic drugs
Prescribed by a kindly psychiatrist and not us, so they must be ok right they must?

My brother is lost to me
Lost to everyone
Buried underneath a rubble eternally
Entirely
Life alongside genetics conspired to be
That much harder for him than me

Tranquillised
Doubled in size

No trouble though my father opines
Yeah, that's half the problem though, right?

He don't talk back
He'll just nod and say yes
An affirmative action
Pavlovian
Learned through years of maladaptive acts
These are just plain as day
Nose on your face facts
Honesty like bullets you can't bite back
You can't write back

Dial back
Undo
Or take back

I'm honestly not sure who I feel sorrier for
My parents having a schizophrenic son
Bloated and bruised with zero views
A ball of anxieties
With a head full of old news

Nostalgia in Sepia toned tinted half truths
Personal propaganda projected onto the walls of his brain
The only time a smile might enter the frame
When he's taking a stroll back down through the good old days

My brother stuck forever with mother and father
Being spoke at
Water boarded with bullshit

Nothing but a blunt hammer in a tool kit
The truth is
We left Aid behind in 1985

And he's still there now living his life
10 years old chasing his friends through the cornfields
A pudding bowl haircut
His smile horizon wide
Pound signs in his eyes

His teeth gleaming white
With his little brother by his side
Jumping from the slide
The smell of freshly cut grass in our noses
Everything coming up roses

As we throw A-Team shapes and Knight Rider poses
It's all 'Look In' magazines
Starsky and Hutch on the TV
Dukes of Hazard
The Fall Guy and family
Just before God came calling for me ...

We were never close
But there was a time
When we were in each other's lives
The most
Shared a bedroom
Played football
You taught me how to ride my bike
Me wobbling unsteady and you running by my side
Once we were entwined

Like brothers

Tied together
Will it be like this forever?
You dreamed of having kids of your own one day
And never, no never did I think
This would be your fate
And we would sever
With such a whimper

Even though you were aloof, and I never felt loved or even liked by you
I still stand by you
You needed something more
Like I did too

Dad's penance is to keep talking to you
Hoping he'll get through to you
Never mind that he missed his chance
And some things we don't get to undo

We have written it down in indelible ink in the hearts of our kids
We don't get to simply erase this
Cos' we realised too late the mistakes that forced this
And maybe it's the right reaction
To feel slightly guilty about this

But don't point the finger at yourself only
What about the glaring gleaming white elephant in the room

The God you chose

It was always a creation
In your mind
A dream you had where you were someone special
Someone alive

And now Aid gets to be at best
A man without the symptoms of psychosis
The elephant sitting on his chest
With all love of music, Tottenham, and the rest
Lost or left

And the madness LPs sit unplayed
Gathering dust
While everything else that he ever loved starts to rust

For this they were never made.
For this life he was never made.

Mislaid
Misplaced

Gone
without a trace.

The act of choosing is the act of losing.

There are so many things that I'll never be

There are so many things that I'll never be

I won't get to be a professional footballer, or an athlete
Open my own chain of restaurants
Or live in the Australian outback and go to work on horseback

I won't go into politics, be an electrician or mend fences for a living

I'll never start my own church in the 1800s in the American south
I'll never be on the cover of time magazine
Buy a big fuckin house

Be a millionaire philanthropist
Or god forbid start a tech company

I'll never be a Priest
Or a Scientist
Or an Astrophysicist
A Nutritionist

I'll never have my own vineyard in rural Sicily
Be friends with George Clooney

Or be a Fisherman in Greece
And grow old and ruddy
My face turning into red leather slowly
I'll never be a Doctor or a Nurse

Or a Deep-sea diver
Or a Long-distance lorry driver

I don't think I'll
Travel too far
Or be a TV star

But I will be a father
A husband
A son
A brother
A friend
A poet
A musician
A social worker

A good man
I won't be everything

But I'll be something
Being something means not being something else

Choosing means gaining and losing
There are roads I'll never walk

That's ok
I'll be somebody

Till the day I drift away
Like an old dandelion being blown out and wished away

And be forgotten like everyone else

And that's ok too
There are some things I'll never be

But forgotten
Isn't one of them

FYI is usually just attached to emails with nothing more said, so I thought it would be funny to write a very long and rambling poem which encompasses all of my thoughts about a whole bunch of things titled FYI

FYI

FYI
OCD
Doesn't stand for
Obsessive
Cleaning
Disorder

And FYI
FYI doesn't stand for
First class
Yeti
Installation

Not everyone with Autism has special abilities
Schizophrenia is not having a split personality
And borderline personality disorder is not getting too attached to your best friend and wanting them all to yourself
Mental illness is not some cutesy character quirk
Schizophrenia is a hammer that smashes your brain into
Teeny
Tiny
Shards

Sugar doesn't make kids hyper
Children getting Ill is necessary and important and not a thing to be avoided

The good old days weren't so good
If there is a celebrity you have an irrational hatred of, well ... they probably hate you too

Everyone on planet earth is addicted to their phones
Adults don't know better than children, they are just more experienced at getting things wrong

And Children don't know better just by virtue of being young
Old people are not always wise or nice

Let's start disliking young children and liking teenagers instead and see what happens
Socially acceptable drugs cause more harm than the ones we fight wars over

There are certain intractable problems in life that we don't know how to fix

Culture always leans left
Government always leans right

Culture reflects society
Not the other way round

Maybe Government leans right because it has to deal with the messy business of ruling
While culture rings its hands makes daisy chains and

sings kumbaya

Religion used to wield its power with impunity, and it still would if it could

It is toothless
Spayed

Because we have pulled its teeth out and cut off its nuts with the bolt cutters of good sense
Logic
And science

There will always be lost people looking for someone to follow
And there will always be bad men willing to lead

I don't care if you did like the Queen
The continued existence of the Royal Family is a moral war crime

The pandemic showed us all what the welfare system is and should be
A safety net for times of deep uncertainty
But we all have short attention spans and faulty memories

The conservatives believe in the markets, in business, in the neo liberal idea of the self. Of never-ending growth, of trickle-down politics of excessive greed and wealth

It was this that caused the 2008 worldwide market

crash and who fronted up the cash??
The poor, the disabled. How do you exactly spell murder?

AUSTERITY

The modern-day Jack the Ripper
Is the Conservative Party

Slashing
And
Gutting
And cutting public services to reduce the deficit like it was a credit card bill

The Tories seized the narrative and they won. They won

13 years. Labour. What have you been up to eh?
Jeremy Corbyn was elected from the grass roots, while Tories were telling the workshy to pull up their boots

JC hated by both left and right, fascinating when both sides come together to fight a common enemy

The Guardian and the Telegraph lining up to toe the party line
When push comes to shove
They always do
See the Iraq invasion, Afghanistan, and Libya too.

As soon as you realise that politics is about keeping

things exactly the same it all makes sense
It's never about change

It's never about change

Despite everyone being against him
JC somehow got elected but he wasn't enough of a
snake to master the black arts and made a mistake
with his take on the antisemitism claims

Yes, the Tories seized upon it and made merry hell
but there was still something to it, it wasn't just
nothing.

Left and right have become splintered
Culture wars are fomented and fought on both sides
Some of them with a sliver of truth
Some outright lies
But all far too serious to be tossed like grenades
For clicks
Likes
And baying moos at PMQ's

Journalism is very nearly dead
A vulture picking at the discarded bones of social
media content

Bands from 25 years ago headline all the major
festivals
In 30 year's time there will be no new music
Just reunion shows
Remakes
And re-boots

Retakes
And reshoots

Everyone should delete Twitter
It's boiling our brains

I want to create
Art for art's sake
But I've still got an ego
And I love a compliment or 2
Flattery and validation
Are not above my station

I've never tasted success
I don't know how I'd cope
I'm better being a normal bloke

But I need to create and not feel like my brains
clucking and stuttering strung out on dope

This feels good

To create and for it to just be enough

And for me to be enough too

Just
You know ...

FYI

To be able to open up to others is a beautiful thing.

The flower

The flower blooms but once a year
The people come to whoop and cheer
With plastic grins from ear to ear
They fight with elbows to get near

The flower is encased in glass
To save its fragile parts
It would wither into dust
If you stole a furtive glance

The stem is London tower block sky
Its petals clamped in a closed fist tight
Radiating a glowing white
Incandescent with atomic sunlight

Cut from glass and bone
of moonlight and stone

It sat alone

As the sunlight started to fade
And dusk mingled with the day

A hush grew in the crowd
Chests rose and fell in unison

As the fist uncurled

A burst of blues
Azure
Cyan
And aqua

And purples
Magenta
Mulberry
And crimson

The gasps came from their eyes
As they were bathed in indigo light

It was over in seconds

But the crowd stayed long into the night

Hoping and praying for a return of the light

The story of your birth.

A joker just like me

13 years ago
I didn't know you
You were waiting
As we were too

I rolled over at 3am
And had a coughing fit
And thought I'd better
Shut up
Because the c section was booked in
For first thing in the morning

I fell asleep
Then woke to find
Your mum
My wife

At the foot of the bed
Unable to talk
Motioning with barely audible sounds
You it seemed
Were in the departure lounge

I flew out of bed
Like a spider monkey
With 18 legs
Grabbed my keys
And raced through the dimly lit quiet of town

To pick up my mum
To come and be with my oldest
I arrived back to the house
In record time
Faster than the speed of light

I called 999 and they said
Brace for impact
So I put a pillow
On the floor between your mum's legs
To soften the blow

I thought
If you fell out
Would the cord act
Like a bungee rope?

The paramedics
Came and trooped up the stairs
'Who put that pillow there?'
I just sheepishly stared

Your mum shut her eyes terrified
And was ferried by blue light
Into the maternity room
Perfect white

I was there too
Not sure what to do
The nurses gave me pom poms
To coax and encourage you

They said to dab your mums head with a flannel
But a lifetime of caution and hesitant indecision paid off
She just wanted to be left alone

After a few strains
Screams
And squeezes

I saw a smudge of ginger
Of crushed amber
A light dusting of Wotsits
On a tiny smooth peanut

So ..
A ginger

In that moment I plucked a name from the
Sky

For the new apple of my eye

I sat and cradled you
Stared into shut eyes
You were here
Tiny and alive

I wondered who you'd be
Like
Your mum
Or like me?

And then the answer

Came to me
As you
Shit all over me

Ahhh
You'll be joker too

Just like me

Why do we wait until someone's dead to tell them what they meant.

Eulogy for the living

Our calloused fingers
Our bloody bones
And broken noses

Our pennies
Our stinky copper eulogies
Tossed absent minded into the well

At wakes for mates
The funeral gates

Straight to hell

The cremation smoke billows
Like the priest's robes
Is god this jolly in the face of death?

We can't know

We are itching for the wake
The tin men oiling up with booze
Tan carpets beer mats and the pokies

The eulogies start to fall
Like ice on a warm windscreen
Words stuck forever in between

Hands find backs
And the scruff of necks
Eyes glaze over
While they gaze over
Each other

They bring out their pennies
Hold them up to the light

Like a eulogy
Only dared said

When drunk

Or dead

Coming to a theatre near you

The Tories on tour

The Tory conference
Is like going to see your dads favourite band from the 60s

Cranking out the big hits
The ones you can easily bop along with
Just ignore the lyrics
It was a different time
Every pop star was a paedophile
And it was fine

The Tories crank out the big hits
The ones they've been transfixing the nation with

'Immigration is out of control '
'Family is under attack '
'We love the gays, but the transgenders need to step back '
'Schools are trying to brainwash your kids'
'Labour will bring socialism and take you to the gulags'
'Climate change is myth '
'Free speech and common sense '
'For Honest, hardworking people '

All of it spilling out of the mouth
Of a billionaire
So removed from the reality of life

He might aswell be living in a gold-plated mansion on the moon

'We need to stand up and fight'
One of them says

Fight?

Like the Tories are some sort
Of plucky underdog
A troubled kid from the streets
Shadow boxing
And skipping

*'You got heart kid, but you're not ready yet '*says the wizened and grizzled seen it all trainer

They are literally the party of government

I'm not one for sound bites

But can we please get these fucking pricks out.

I love my dad's vulnerability

A fleeting moment of honesty

His voice is small
Cracked
Telling me things
I already know

This conversation
Like much of our correspondence
On a one-way radio

With suicidal thoughts
Missed chances
Regrets
Guilt
Tragedy
And honesty

May be
The most authentic moment we've shared

That's why I love the bleak
It's true
It's honest

It's oddly comforting
To hear you speak the truth
Cos there's many things I don't know

But one thing I do know

Is you

For Rio, the original butterscotch brother.

2 things my dog hates. Pigeons and Postman

My dogs pure and unadulterated
Weapons grade hatred
For the Royal Mail
Stems largely from his
Proud working class
Anti-monarchist roots

A student of history
He may be
Fully aware of the villains and their mendacity
The oppressive iron glove of the aristocracy

But his real ire
Springs from the time
A parcel fell from the letterbox
And landed on his head

And from that day forward
Every time he sees a flash of red
Through concave glass
He unleashes a volley of barks
That seem to say
'*I can forgive the past*
With all its sophistry

But I can't forget the scars
Or the stars I saw

And from this day forward there will always be a war
That lasts more than 100 lifetimes
And if I somehow sire a child
Even though my testicles have long ago expired
I'll pass the baton onto him

To carry it on and never bow his head to cower or play dead
In the face of such tyranny
As a parcel falling onto thee '

Pigeons remind him
Of his brief sojourn
On the streets of Trafalgar Square
Trying to make it as a beat poet and failing

Cos even though he can rock a beret with the best of them
And Bukowski and Ginsberg were contemporaries as well as fans

He had no hands
Couldn't hold a pen
And his poetry fell from his lips
In barks and growls

He hit the booze hard
And slept rough in the square
Under the shadow of Westminster
And he was woken every morning by the fluttering wings of those dammed things
And their incessant cooing

So, he chased them all away
Every single one
And headed home
Joined the family business after all
And forgot about his love of Kerouac and Corso

So, when he sees one now
Resplendent in funereal gray
He's taken back to those heady and glorious days
The dimly lit smoky bars
The excitement
The activism
The freedom of the pen
And finding his tribe
His friends

And how it was all shat on
From an almighty height
By life's great pigeon

God himself

So, I guess this poem should be titled

3 things my dog hates
Pigeons, postman

and god

We care about the wrong things.

Small boats vs the Tories live on Sky Sports

Perhaps the small boats carrying desperate parents and kids
'Migrants' to use the current parlance

Should play the theme tune to Match Of The Day when they are bouncing and bobbing among the waves

With commentary by Guy Mowbray

And serious northeast half time analysis by Alan Shearer

And the migrants should be clad in the colours of our favourite football teams
The Chelsea blues
Arsenal reds
With names emblazoned on the back of them

And the crossings should be televised on Sky Sports
With swooping swishing quick cut camera angles

And if we keep doing it for 50 years

Then the dusty sepia toned nostalgia of our new national game may trigger some kind of new National shame

And we'll care more for strangers on boats dying in the sea

Than the sport equivalent of strictly

But
Will we?

Will we?

No

Cos' the theme tune to Match Of The Day has been seared into our brains
Setting off memories
Sparking off molecules
And particles
Lighting up
And firing up
Dreams of youth
John Motson's excitement
At Ray Wilkins curling strike

'That's absolutely magnificent!'

I can feel the smile
In my bones
In my feet
Cutting through all the misery
In 1985
Norman Whiteside
That curling strike

That classic red kit
And the company that sponsored it

And our game has been tainted
The new plaything
Of the mega rich
Sport washing

That new 100-million-pound signing might aswell be
Drenched in blood

People died to build a stadium
For millionaires to kick a ball around
But I still cheered when we got to the second round

How?
Dissonance I guess
Ignorance is bliss

Match Of The Day
The migrant boats
Vs the Tories

I need to read their stories
Maybe then I'll care enough
To act
Instead of saying the right things online

And getting clicks and likes
And feeling warm and fuzzy inside

Those people in the small boats

Trying to stay afloat

Just trying to stay afloat
A punchline to a joke

A subject of a poem I wrote
A tweet

A Facebook link
A footnote

Our obsession with romance has bred many a stalker and broken up many a marriage.

I wanna be mine

I don't wanna be yours
I don't wanna be his or hers
I don't wanna be the body in the open top hearse
The faded yellow photo in your red leather purse
The vow mouthed at the altar 'for better or worse' like a curse

I don't wanna be your tearful apology or your fingertip bruise
I don't wanna be your muse
I wanna be the whole vintage cabinet not just the screws

I wanna be mine
I wanna be the first taste of sweet amber nectar in the sunshine
I wanna be the water that turns into wine
I wanna be the face of Jesus Christ seared into a ham and cheese toastie on rye

On a 2 out of ten day I wanna be a 9
I wanna be the first flush of love, that bashful awkward smile
I wanna be the extra mile
The open horizon stretching out wild

I wanna be alive

And not just in your eyes
Not growing only in your gaze
Be my own trend and craze
My own tsunami wave
Not slapping on a brave face
But for it to be true
And feel the love deepest darkest blue

I wanna be mine

A well educated and elected member of government in 2023 described homelessness as a lifestyle choice. I kid you not.

Lifestyle choice

I don't know about you
But sometimes I get a bit sick of central heating
Of my front and back door
Of my carpets
My laminate floor

I just get bored of

My corner sofa
And my big screen TV
My fridges, oven, and microwave
My draw of cutlery
my mugs, glasses of varying sizes
Pints, pitchers, shot glasses, all chalices for my vices

I've had my fill of

My wretched curtains that keep the light out and the warmth in
My guitars that hang like severed deer heads on a plinth

My photos
Of my grinning kids
Sun kissed in Corfu

Sea hair all askew

I cannot abide my bed
With its memory foam mattress that fits perfect with this pig's bladder on a stick head

My double duvet
My wardrobe of clothes, t shirts, jeans, hoodies, a pair of pointed court jester mustard shoes

I've had it up to here with

My box fresh vans that look so cool
Trademark maroon
Trademark maroon blisters too!

My toothbrush
Toothpaste
Warm water from the tap
Splashed across my face
Deodorants
Both underarm and spray
And some barely ever used aftershave

My piping hot power shower
My comfy towels
Ahhhhh My beautiful boiler

Sometimes I think, you know what

'Fuck it!'

It's time for a change

A lifestyle choice
I'll sleep under a bit of damp canvas
And get addicted to spice
I'll beg for money on a cobbled stone street
Huddle in a doorway like a shadow with teeth

Sit so close to the ground
That even 5-year-olds tower over me
Have no friends
And no family

Rely on the kindness of strangers
Chucking me some shrapnel
Or a buying me a coffee

Have literally no money

Lose all sense of space and time
Minutes drag, days sag, and years fly

Die an early death
25 years before the rest
Succumbing to the cold
Around the years end

The sound of the carollers
The twinkling of the lights
The shoppers laden down with bags
The brittle and brutal nights

I wonder why no one ever made a TV show about this lifestyle choice

I wonder why?

I wonder why

(Epilogue)

Sue Ellen Braverman
You were named after a character from Dallas
It's like your parents almost knew
You'd end up an absurd caricature
A cartoon

No one chooses to be homeless
But if they did

It would still make more sense
Than choosing to be

A Tory

One of my finest moments as a father

Fuck them

Daughter dressed to impress at her school disco
Black skinny jeans, shirt, and tie
The emo apple of my eye

The boys mocked her
Called her emo
She cried
Sat outside

(How very emo)

After the hugs and the consoling kindness
Abated
I said there will always be dickheads in this world
For that fact we are fated
But we gotta gird ourselves up to make it

We can't always shape it
But we can shake it
Fake it till we break it

So, repeat the mantra
After me
Repeat the mantra
1, 2, 3

Fuck them

Fuck their puny tiny minds
Consumed with the ordinary
The mundane banal times

Fuck their replica football kits
Those arrogant little shits
From cities they've never even visited

Fuck their jokes and TikTok views
Fuck their empty-headed banter
And their old news

Fuck their treacle thick machismo
Their inability to let anyone just be

Fuck their mums and dads and their generational idiocy

Fuck them all

Repeat it every day
Until It's chiselled into your brain in a permanent way

Fuck them

Never ever let them or anyone get in your way

Fuck them
I say

Fuck everyone

Who ever tries to make you feel small
Once and for ever all

Repeat after me

'Fuck them'

You know who this is about (allegedly, allegedly)

Open secrets, invertebrates, and fundamentalist Christian's

Once again
A prominent celebrity
Is exposed

As not just a grifter
A charlatan
A wannabe Bodhisattva

But an **alleged** sex offender

Leaving a trail of ruin
In his wake
Hiding in plain sight
In the smoke
Of lacquered hair
And risqué jokes

And as the tide turns
And it's clear his millions won't save him

Then

And only then

Actors and comics peak their heads out
And talk of open secrets
And private WhatsApp groups

Of furtive glances
Whispers
Of the truth

But they decided to save their own skins
Instead of standing for something
And yeah, he's litigious and powerful

But you knew it was happening
And you said nothing

This is the tie that binds all scandals together
The Boston lawyer who sued the Catholic Church said

'If it takes a village to raise a child, it takes one to abuse it'

He was once a drug addict
Then a shock comic
A shagger
And then bizarrely
A modern-day Che Guevara

Telling tales of revolution
In a cravat on Newsnight
By turns charismatic and erudite

But he also wore a cape and a cowboy hat
To a commons committee
So still kind of a wanker obviously

After a time, he left the left
The pandemic turned his head
Swivelled it on a stick
And it was strange to see who he was now rubbing shoulders with

And now
All the right-wing YouTubers
Who he's been cosying up to

Come flying to his defence
With talk of due process and the rest

Hey, imagine he's a drag artist
Then you'd be able to locate your outrage

But cos he bleeds blue
They are falling over themselves
To avoid the truth

Here's just one of his defenders

Matt Walsh

He cares so much about women,
he, in a thinly veiled piece of crypto homophobia for the 2020s
Did a whole documentary trying to find out 'what is a woman'?

But there was no need for the film
I could have saved him the time
A woman is a baby making machine who needs to

get in the kitchen and make Matt Walsh some pie

When Roe v Wade was overturned
He tweeted that we should drink up and 'enjoy the leftist tears'
As if this was all just some game

The conspiracy theorists are now sharpening their keyboards
'He's been silenced
They've finally come for him'

One YouTube comment compared him to Julian Assange

As far as I can remember
Julian Assange didn't present Big Brother's Big Mouth and think of endlessly childish names for his winkie

And get sacked by the BBC for upsetting the waiter from faulty towers
And after a lifetime of promiscuity and sex jokes

Reinvent himself as a wellness guru, cult leader come life coach
Dress in flowing robes

No, he's banged up in Belmarsh

Because If you are a real threat to the establishment

You don't see them coming

The truth is
We should not deify any celebs
We do not know them

The real heroes of the world are nameless
Not famous

Anyway
At least this time

They caught a live one

I guess that's progress

Someone said 'indifference is chilling' but I don't know who

A shrug is a silent shove

A shrug is sometimes worse than a shove
Indifference is like bleeding to death in a library

You can hear a pin drop
But not a tear drop

Apathy
Marinates in the memory

And memories make me
Me

Indifference
Is like travelling in separate cars

Mine is on fire
And I can see you listening to the radio

I beep my horn and wave
I can see your lips move

Who are you talking to?
You have a mannequin in the front seat

With Gaffa tape on its mouth
You are dressed smart in a suit

Apathy is the perfunctory rituals
Handshakes

Yearly texts
Getting drunk and slapping me on the back

Apathy is living in a space station
Sending emails describing how the earth looks and how you feel close to god now

Apathy is being a donator of sperm
Leaving a baby on a doorstep of an orphanage

Simply giving life is enough
Like god did for us

Apathy is holding someone at arm's length and dropping them because it hurts your arm

'Holding you, hurt my arm, hurt me...
You hurt me '

So now I'm orbiting mercury
My spaceship is covered in ice

Because nothing can live here
This to me feels more painful than nothing at all

So, I'll say goodbye
To apathy

Indifference
To family

To fathers and mothers
And love

A shrug is a silent shove

This is the truest fiction.

The elephant

Once, when I was 5
My dad brought home an elephant
My mum was not pleased

'What's he going to eat, where's he going to sleep?'

She politely enquired

'Don't worry it will be fine, this elephant is just what this family needs '

The elephant was small, and no trouble at all
He curled up in the dog's bed
Wrapped and nestled in his own trunk and slept

I noticed small changes
My dad's car key was now attached to a cartoon elephant
There was a scented elephant wearing a baseball cap that hung from dad's rearview mirror
But it smelled of lemons not elephants

And he bought us elephant T shirts which he insisted we wore every day to school

My friend Dean said
'Dude, what's with the elephants?'

I shrugged and said '*I dunno, it's my dad's thing*'

My dad started dressing in funereal grey

Grey suits
Grey socks and boots
Grey oversized pants
Grey shirts buttoned all the way up
A grey hat on top

'*What's up with dad?*' I said to mum

She shook her head
'*He's always been a strange one*'

The elephant seemed content to snooze his days away, but too big for the dog bed, he now slept on the sofa instead

One day dad called me downstairs as he had something for me
I trotted down the stairs eagerly
Dad was sitting down cradling the elephant
Rubbing its belly
And making baby noises

He stopped as I entered and gestured with his head
To a present carefully wrapped in grey wrapping paper

'*What is it?*' I said with a smile

My excitement was matched by my fathers
'Open it, open it '

I hurriedly tore apart the paper and my face fell into a befuddled and puzzled frown
My dad's grin remained fixed to his face even wider than before

I picked the present up between finger and thumb

They were elephant ears

'Dad what are these?'

'Elephant ears for school'
'Just THINK how happy it will make him '

The elephant stared at me with fixed unreadable eyes which were a match for mine.

From that day on, me and my siblings wore elephant ears every day at school

We were called the dumbo kids and the children would throw peanuts and wave their arms like a trunk and pretend to fly and blow raspberries in our eyes

My best friend Dean turned his back on me, said he couldn't play with me anymore, he couldn't be friends with the dumbo kid

'Just take them off' he implored ..

but I couldn't
Dad had glued them to my head

The elephant grew while mum withdraw
Dad changed the living room into a mini zoo
Straw and giant water bowls the elephant's trunk sloshed around
My toys trodden down
Han Solo and Luke skywalker covered in elephant poo
I scrubbed them with an old toothbrush as you do

The stench clung to our clothes and followed us everywhere we'd go

One day dad sat us down for a family meeting
He told us that our finances were depleting
The elephant was costing us big bucks
And stupid foolish me got my hopes up
And thought this meant the elephants time was up

But no

'You all have to get jobs 'dad said

'You'll give up school and start contributing'

'But dad, I can't work I'm 7 years old, I don't want to have an elephant, I never wanted one, none of us did, we were happy before, please, please just get rid '

My dad frowned and said I was selfish and how

many kids my age would dream of having an elephant. I just stared.

Me and my siblings got odd jobs doing peoples gardens around town and the elephant continued to grow

My dad became known as the guy with the elephant
He'd ride him around
Telling folks what a great pet they are, and everyone should get one too

But they just laughed
They knew
It was a stupid thing to do
And to do to your kids too

One day mum finally snapped
And told my dad
It's us or the elephant you choose

But dad would not be moved
This was who he was now
The guy with the elephant
He tried his best to remember why he brought it home in the first place, but he couldn't

He went to bed
With the elephant sitting on his chest
In a loving caress
He'd done this since he was a baby but now, it weighed a tonne maybe

The elephant crushed my dad's heart and his lungs and by morning he had ran out of breath

In his will he bequeathed to us all his worldly possessions, his guitar, his adidas vests, but his greatest treasure of all he gave to me

'Leon, the elephant is for you. You must tend to it, feed it, pet it and need it. It will help you through life. Let him always be your guide. I know you'll take good care of it '

Do you know there are people who believe that the Daily Mail is an actual newspaper.

Daily hate mail: A public service announcement

I consider the cartoon rag akin to a 1950s comic
The Beano
The Dandy
The Daily Mail

We had stacks of them in our cupboard under the sink and we used it
To line our hamster cages
To soak up the piss and shit

And as I watched the piss and shit soak into the bold newsprint
The clouds parted
And the sun beamed down from the heavens
With a voice booming out saying
'This surely is a blessed union'

I thought surely nobody takes seriously
The shit spun endlessly

But so obviously that you could set your clock to it

In the Daily Mail

But I saw a boys charity post a link to an article in it
And I wanted to wail

And I know the Daily Mail is low hanging fruit
But for anyone that reads it this is for you

As a public service
To spread awareness
I present to you
The following tool
As a barometer
A measuring rule
Daily mail bingo

The good ole days.
Women are whores.
White supremacy of course.
Bloody immigrants.
Sex scandals.
Mills and boon tone in reporting said sex scandals.
Hasn't this female celebrity got fat and old.
The poor are a feral festering boil that needs lancing.
A quisling lickspittle for Queen and empire.
Sponging benefits claimants.
Barely disguised contempt for LGBTQ+.
Climate change denial and contempt for activism.
An outright hatred of the young unless its young men accused of rape.
Anti-black footballers.
Bashing the BBC!
An overall tone of sneer, leer, and sanctimony.

So next time you think of sharing some anonymous

story of boys being me-tooed to death remember the rotten stench of this list
And maybe pool all your money and collectively burn every copy of this rag instead

Its actually all year round.

Games I play with my family at Christmas

My mum and I
play a game
Similar to *'guess who?'*

It's called *'guess who's dead'*
The rules are my mum has to tell me about someone who I don't know who has died
And I have to pretend to care

My dad and I pick up the pieces on the game we've been playing for my whole life
Called *'will he ever ask me a personal question?'*

'And would I even know what to say if he did '

My sister and I play Cluedo, she tries to murder me with the lead pipe in the library and I have to solve the murder myself while my mum and dad try to cover it up

My younger brother and I play battleships where he fires missiles and tries to sink my ship with my wife and kids in it.

My older brother and I pull a cracker and there is pink party hat inside, and he smiles like it's the best thing that's happened to him in years.
Happy Christmas

Love is about making a pact with the unknown. With whatever is coming down that road

A new name

My child says they want to change their name

They don't fit anymore
With the one I gave

On the day they were born
The first thing I saw
Was a smudge of red
Atop their head

And it grew
Into rolling, ringlets
Of autumnal hue

Rivulets
Of crushed amber
And marigold

And the name used to fit you
Like a woollen mitten
On a smoky November night

But now
Your curls cut short
Your hair the colour of a starless sky

Sombre

The weight of the world
On your little shoulders

It's not right
It doesn't matter

I'll still be
What I've always tried to be

The caretaker of your heart
So, farewell 'Abby'

And hello
'Alex'

Try asking 'what were you like as a child?' the next time you are meeting someone new. Never again ask someone what they do for work.

The best years of your life

Most grown ups
Suffer from an affliction
An insidious
Predilection
For fiction

A collective amnesia
A rose-tinted anaesthesia
Glinting
Gleaming
Like drops of LSD
On a bloodshot eyeball

None more delusional than Childhood

Now children ...

Being a grow up kind of blows
You gotta pay bills
Fill out your tax return
Clean your house
Pumice the dry skin off your toes

Care for sick and ailing parents
Watch yourself get old and creaky
And see popular culture disappear further

Over the horizon with every passing year

A reminder of your lost youth
This uncomfortable truth
As must as it's possible now to stave it off
With fillers and Botox

Ice baths and eating clean
Park runs gaming
Listening to 6 music
And trying to get into modern bands
The truth is
It's all slipping through your hands

Time

That thing we feel is endless
Isn't
As soon as we open our eyes
That first few cries
We are all of us
Starting to die

(And I can feel you roll your eyes and that's the point right)

We know this
But we can't cope with this
So, we catapult this as far as we can see
All the way to the lemon trees on mercury

But when we see children
We set off a homing beacon

And this thought flies straight back
With the almighty crack
Of a baseball hitting a bat

And we deify them first
As magical super beings
And it's all firsts

First cries
First tufts of hair
First steps
First words
First teeth
First loves
First of a million hugs

By the time they reach the cusp of teenage hood
This magic has all run out

It's like the fall of man in Genesis
Or the movie Gremlins

Take your pick

So, we, armed with all this knowledge of every
moment that's ever passed us
Start to hate kids
Because they remind us of everything
We've ever lost
And they don't appear to know what they have

So, we start to spout sound bites
Like we always used to hate

Like *'school is the best years of your life'*
And *'you don't know your born mate'*

And we read the Daily Mail and start to look for the evidence that THIS is the worst generation of kids that's ever lived!

And yes, there may be evidence

Because this is the first generation to have their every move and every word, and every passing fleeting foolish farting thought documented

We have created an archive
Of miscellaneous
Missteps
And
Mistakes
To shame
Shake and berate

But to be a child
Is to be a sort of open-air prisoner
Pushed from lesson to lesson
Tested
Compared
Marked and stamped with a tag
And made to stand over there

A bunch of tiny human beings in a place
All just trying to get through
Be the bully or the bully's mate
Or sporty

Or cool
Or an emo or a goth
Wear black

And get asked about your self-harm scars
As if it's all such a laugh

'Cut my life into pieces! This is my last resort!'
Hahahahahaha

There really is nothing more amusing than
emotionally suffering

Childhood is brutal

And this is just the western version
Our construction
Confection
It's all a delusion

So, when adults say to kids
You don't know how easy you've got it

What they are really saying is

Its shit being a grown up

Don't do it

My version of the tiger came to tea

Cancer for tea

I invited cancer round for tea
I felt sorry for it
It gets such a bad rap
People always talking smack

We had a few bevvies
And I thought
'This guy's alright you know, a dark sense of humour I like that '

Bet then his eyes twinkled as he regarded me
And he devoured me whole

Cancer, it turns out

Is a c*** after all

Imagine the indignity of peaking in high school

The cool kid

The most popular kid in school
6 feet tall
15 years old
Sideburns and stubble

The girls all in thrall
Giggling and bashful
Head tilts and longing smiles
Love notes love letters
Little love hearts that stretch for miles

Flashing a sovereign ring
A birthday present from his Dad
Dreaming of being a pro footballer
Trials for Ipswich town and West Ham

Running out for football
Boots clacking on the concrete
Growing in the pack
The shoal of cool kids
The footballers

The class of 1995
Me just one of the onlookers
Flash forward 27 short years

I am walking my dogs
It's autumn

Sodden cherry red leaves gather underneath
Scorched and bare trees
Natures pot pouri

Lazy rainfall
Soaks everything to the skin
The sky drooping down like fog
Mingling

Past the football pitch behind the fence
Sunday league kids
I see an old guy eye me
Puffy faced
Paunchy of frame
Squashed and squeezed into a puffer jacket

It's the cool kid
Of Bramston school fame

Coaching Sunday league

The opposition have a corner
The ball is flighted over
It bounces over heads and finds a boy named Luca
He swivels on a sixpence and pings it in

The touch line erupts

4-0

'Fucking 4 nil
Fucking joke'

The cool kid spits as he kicks the fence
He folds his arms and leans back

Soaked to the skin
The cool kid

43
Swearing at children
On a sodden sleepy autumn Sunday

Where did it all go wrong?

Pretty self-explanatory this one

The cult kid and me

There was no cult compound
No polygamy
No charismatic preachers
Just weapons grade banality

No water into wine
No manna from heaven
Just traipsing out to the Kingdom Hall Thursdays at half past 7

After dinner I'd lay on my parent's bed watching the doomsday digits of the phone clock
Tick down to 7oclock
Hoping this was a night we'd miss It, and I could finally watch Top Of The Pops

But alas mum would call out and I'd pull on my suit with a sigh and reach for my briefcase
No ten-year-old should even own a fucking briefcase

It was light black plastic
Inside it, a songbook, a beet red Bible, a notepad, and a pen.

Dad would send me and my older brother over early to save some seats
We went straight out the front door, down the

tarmac car park and through the hole in the bushes.
Where we saw 3 buildings
One for scouts
One for sea cadets
And one for cult kids

The scouts were learning how to tie knots and use a compass
The sea cadets were learning how to sail and work as a team
And me?

I was learning that masturbation was evil

I didn't even know what masturbation was
If I'd gone to scouts maybe I'd have found out

While the scouts were learning the lyrics to kumbaya
I was sat in a chair for 2 hours also learning about 'The Lord'
Tell me what you think of this guy

A guy who makes bets with the devil
And cuts down the whole orchard for the sake of some rotten apples
Who sends plagues to prove his 'name'
Who's answer to every question is always kill and kill again
A guy who threw out his first-born kids because they made 1 mistake

They were kids

They didn't know

This is the top guy
The one at the top of the tree
The Old Testament god name of Yahweh
All powerful but kind of petty

We were told to think of this guy as our Heavenly Father
When this is your dad
You grow up seriously confused about love and attachments

You hold everyone at arm's length
As if inspecting them for flaws
Of which there are plenty of course
And when you find a wrinkle which you are surely bound to
You can throw them away
Because you have to

But you don't just hold others up to the light
You do it to yourself
Morning
Noon
And night

This is how you learn
Self-loathing

I was 10
I was a kid

There was no compound
No cache of weapons
No commune
No Kool aid
Well not the kind that kills you straight away mate

I went to school
Out into the world
Every day with a target on my back
Hiding behind my eyes
Watching everyone for signs
Of judgement

I was different from everyone else, and boy did I know it
I was defined by everything I couldn't do

No birthdays
No Christmas
No Easter
No Father's Day
Or mothers
No Valentine's Day
No Halloween
No joining a football team

No
No
No

The cult kid wants love
But doesn't trust it

Being held at arm's reach is all he knows and he's happier with it

The cult kid yearns for the ending of everything
The smell of cordite as the world is burning
Doomsday
The end of the world
Fireballs from heaven
Blood red Armageddon
The last days of this old system

The cult kid is now a man
Doing the best, he can

He made it out

And found his way back home to himself
Hugged his ten-year-old self and told him
'We can work it out'
'You're not alone '
and you're ok.

You always were.'

'Let's walk this road together with complete uncertainty and trust that I'll always be here'

The cult kid and me

The cult kid and me

Here's my dad again

Parker pens

I got gifted some Parker pens
A parting gift from some parting friends
But I'm not one for stylish accoutrements
Cuff links pressed shirts and shined up shoes

No, I'm a scuffed-up converse kid
Ripped jeans checked shirts and shit
I leave the stylish threads to classier men than me
Jordan Peterson and guy Ritchie (ha)

There is one guy though who likes Parker pens
Shined up shoes and high-top boots
My dad
The oldest rebel in town

Cut down slightly to size by radiotherapy
His last dose was this Wednesday
And so, I thought I'd pop in and give them to him
No great gift, after all I did not pay for it

But to see the look on his face as I turned up at his place
You'd be forgiven for thinking that I'd brought more chemo
More radiotherapy
More invasive surgery

He saw me coming and I could see his face darken

into a scowl

'What are you after?'

The words hissed from his lips like smoke
My heart slumps slightly as it should do rightly

He really is a strange bloke

I shake my head and roll my eyes like freshly loaded dice
But I'm not surprised as this is what my dad is just *like*

I hand over the box
He shifts it in his fingers but can't work out how it unlocks
Much like his own heart

He gathers himself and tells me the doctors have left permanent damage
How he wished he'd never had it
Human vivisection and those 'bastard doctors' planned it

He is slightly slurry so half in the bag probably
After all it is a Friday
He tells me he has bought a brand-new microphone
and I remember his goal of singing Irish folk tunes

He claws his way back to himself and says he has something for me
The irony

Of seconds earlier being annoyed at the presence of me
Thinking I'd come with my hand out and now he's rushing inside to get me something
He disappears and comes back with microphone leads

Still in the cellophane
I take them, he taps me on the shoulder
I leave him to his muddy thoughts and melancholy slumber

The leads will stay wrapped in plastic and thrown in a draw and I'll find them long after he's gone and no more

I'll stare at them and remember how he was
Not how I wanted him to be

The malfunctioning head of my malfunctioning family

For Sinead O'Connor

The artists manifesto

Poetry should not be written on the side of buildings
It should be written in blood and smeared on our naked chests
It should be shouted into the faces of passers-by
Bellowed from rooftops

It will not, should not, cannot ever lie
Which is why it should not ever be used to advertise
The paid lies we imbibe

Is there a more pitiful sight
Than a punk
Pathetically parroting a poem
2 subcultures co opted
By corporate vultures

The poem
Written by a panel
To sell us insurance when
We travel

Poetry should not be written in the lobbies of corporate businesses
It should be scruffily spray painted
In subways and underground trains
And the poets should be chased
By overweight
Out of shape

Security guards on minimum wage

Not stencilled prettily
In our brand-new metro cities
As proof of culture
Not stitched onto cushions
And sold on Etsy

It should not be pretty
Or twee
Or even funny

Yeah, I know I'm describing all my back catalogue

But allow me
a moment of sincerity

To say what an artist
should be

And If the price you pay for being one
Is having a day job then so be it

Better that than selling out
And running writing retreats in Longleat

Poetry should make you gasp
Take your breath away
Should make you feel something
It should disturb

In the lord's words

'I came to bring a sword'

Write
Always

With a pure and dangerous heart
That would really be something

That would be a start

Words sometimes fail us

What to say?

What to say?
When you write
You can't do life

Can't go on
'I am done'

With weary resignation
You've only known 12 summers
But you must have suffered

In some invisible way
One you cannot say
Hair once vibrant

Now Tim Burton black
A star lost
In a pale winter sky

A narrowing of the eyes
I know that look
I've felt it curl around my spine

Dull the colour in my eyes
I know the taste of thick gloom
Of smoke

What to say?

When you feel this way
There's nothing

It's all been said anyway
By all the writers
Of all the symphonies

The novellas
The architects of pain and poetry
The songs that ride your optic nerve

Leave chem-trails up your spine
Saying 'you are not the first'
There must be some worth

In sticking around
To hear the music

You are not the only one to hear it

You are not the only one to hear it

For Mark, the guy who saved my life.

Death by orange

I nearly died at 11.25
Under glowing buzzing standard office issue strip lights
In front of a laptop screen
Inputting data
Living the dream

Not surrounded by family
Beloved friends
Cards from well wishers
The kind you hope to never send

I'm opposite a girl I barely know
And she seems nice and all
But if I pop my clogs
I don't want a stranger to be the last one to see me go

I'd wanna be in my bed
Advanced in years
Pondering a life well lead
With a drip line full of beer

On the way to work I'd been listening to the Blind Boy Podcast
With his tips on mental wellness for the new year
He spoke of being mindful
Not ruminating like a cow on the last spin cycle

And as I pulled up at the car park, I marvelled at his
ability to see inside my brain and perfectly articulate
my pain

By 11.25 the thought of Blind boy was long gone, lost
as I was
In the iron grip of the tyranny of the 'to do list '

I pulled out an orange to eat it

There was a little too much give in the peel
I didn't rightly trust it
But I pulled it apart and stuffed a couple of segments
in my mouth
My eyes never once leaving the screen

All was going well until I decided to breathe
The segment skin now shorn of the juicy centre
Was caught by the wind of my inhalation
Like a kite being caught on an ingracious gust of
wind

The kite flew backwards and into my throat and
stuck there
Leaving me gasping for air
Like a plastic bag in a gale
Rippling and shimmering
My eye sockets very nearly popping

I noticed the sound I was making
And I thought

'This is embarrassing '

As I stood from
My chair
Bent double over the desk
Trying to breathe the kite out of there

I could hear commotion around me
Shrieks and classically British concerned looks
And then finally 2 sharp heavy slaps
On my back
Before the orange hit my desk with a splat

Thankfully
I could breathe again
I really wanted to talk
So I could start making light of the incident

On the way home I listened to the second part of
Blind Boy's podcast
Where he closed by talking about how to mindfully
eat an orange

So there you have it

I always knew Blind Boy was a genius but now I also
think he's a prophet
a seer

and very maybe the second coming of Christ

Dog bless

Friendship is one of life's underrated joys

Friends take time

Friends take the time
To know more than the headlines

The footnotes

Not just the broadest of brush strokes
The air kisses and life quotes

'So, life has got you by the throat?'
'Let me show you this song I wrote '

Friends know the structure of your DNA
Not just your birthday
They send lists of things they appreciate
And miss
Not just 'happy birthday' with a kiss

Friends take the time to connect
With no agenda
How did you find your oldest childhood friend?
Standing next to them
In the lunch line
I turned and smiled
And they liked it enough to return it

Friends know how the fabric of your universe feels to touch
Or maybe I'm expecting too much

Find one or 2 who are this for you

Hold them tight to your chest
Never let it rest

Never let them go

Sometimes you can do everything right, prepare well and it still all goes to shit

The worst gig in the history of the world

Like most days
It started off ok
A new day

Sleepy, blinking it emerged into the sun

Nowhere to clock in
Nothing to become

Loose limbed languid and lazy
No ambition to meet
A daydream hazy

A sun-drenched Sunday
Which the birds sung in
A million strong
And I was up shaking hands with the day early
In the mood for collaboration
Fist bumps, back slaps
Ideas way above my station

A dog walk around the farmer's field
A leisurely stroll around my subconscious
All preparation for today's gig

A gig at a festival now, this was something new and exciting

I had my set
I'd done my due diligence
I'd done my prep
I was in sync and step
Between body, brain, and breath

Done my jobs
Made my wife a tea in bed
Kissed my kids
Walked my dogs

Everything set out perfect
In its place
A carefully assembled tower of blocks
A Jenga tower
To hit the rocks

Now it's about logistics
Find Ricci's house
Follow the Sat Nav
Drive the wrong way, turn around
Push one piece of the Jenga tower out

Arrive safely, all roads look the damn same to me
Ricci's out, he's dressed different from me,
fingernails painted red, baggy dungarees and I don't
know why that should bother me but as he's coming
out

With every step
It's pushing out
Another piece of the Jenga tower all the way out

A new postcode in the Sat Nav
Some awkward chit chat
Ricci jokes that he hopes this is not some elaborate kidnapping plan, harvest his organs, leave him cold in the bathtub, that kind of scam
We chuckle as we head deeper into the Essex hinterland

The satellite takes us the bloody wrong way, I guess it must be hard to see from space, but here we are surrounded by cows in a farmer's field (what's that sound? The sound of 2 more holes in the Jenga tower being revealed)

I turn the car around; we move from Sat Nav car to Sat Nav phone

I imagine the tension up in a space that we have switched from one satellite to another, and the rejected one running home to his mother, crying that he never wanted to do this anyway, he wanted to go to art school!

Back down to earth with the earth man and me, handing over our tickets to security and parking up safely and securely with no charge monetary

We head aimlessly towards the vague direction of the main arena, first through cars then through tents, Ricci is all bright eyed and looking for people he knows, in a matter of seconds he's found someone and off he goes

We find the tent where we are performing, grab a beer and I settle down, things turn into a simple Sunday for a while, we watch a band, meet a nice guy called Will and sit on the grass and wait for the time to pass

We amble over to the tent at gig time
A long-haired guy in a DMT fever dream jump suit with loose and wobbly eyes
Tells us it's fine but we are running behind time

I get the sense that he is running on his own clock, it's no great shock, this being day 3 of the festival, Deep into the deepest darkest of psychedelic rabbit holes

However, with each passing minute of delay
Jenga blocks are slowly sliding out of place
They make no sound as they drop this time
They just slip into the black hole of space and time

There is drum and bass pumping from the tent
There is bodies slumped from too much Ket
There is half naked female bodies painted in red
And an awkward ex Christian boy not knowing what to do next

At this point I'm
Sick of waiting and I move across to another tent to see a musician called Bridget
Who I think is brilliant

Sadly, I am tracked down quickly and taken back to

My guillotine
My gallows

The guy on first is in shades
Jittery all nervous energy
Up no doubt for days
Performing a Capella, no page
His words like a machine gun
Scattering bullets
That sometimes hit and more often miss

I try to tune my ear to listen, but he is swaying
between microphone and dead air
And his static crackling energy makes me want to
bolt out of there
He turns his head and delivers his poem
Lastly directly to me
Before stumbling off swaying
Leaving a mass of headless daisies on the floor
decaying

The MC, a half-naked lady trying to coordinate brain
and top and lower half of body
Jerks with stone limbs to the stage
Mumbles something incoherent
Before introducing me with the wrong name

I had planned to do a 20-minute set
I had my poems all written down on my hand
I had my book
I had my plan
But this
None of this was part of it

I didn't want to be late on
I didn't want to perform to this
I'm a massive square I guess
There's me thinking I was somehow cool, but I digress

This is all one big digression
How long before I learn these lessons
Class is in session, and it has been for years
When you gonna finally wake up to your fears and face them, and embrace them instead of chasing them and arranging them
In carefully placed block towers
And acting all surprised when they don't stay standing for hours

The walk towards the stage
Takes an age
I take my book, I find my page
I rattle through a poem
I knew well enough to just fucking say

The poem is personal
Of vulnerability and fear
And I'm here
Right back in the same spot
Let's have ourselves a cheer
(hooray)

I rattle through
I get off in record time

I sit on a bench in the corner
Trying my best not to disappear into a scorched
shadow, the only proof I was here
I know it's good form to sit and listen

So, I do
But the words are just more stimuli
More salt in the wound
Sand in my eye

There's one guy who repeats the same line over and over
Like the ultimate stopped
Doomsday clock

But he did say right at the top
He was shit at poetry
Was it self-deprecation? It was not
Was it honesty? It appears it was

It might have been a good idea to take a step outside
Get some air
Take some time

But I don't

At the end
Ricci seems giddy and happy
Full of trademark puppy dog energy
And I feel guilty for pissing on his parade

So, I suck it all up behind the tightest smile

The one that stretches back so far
That a satellite could track its miles

What of my Jenga tower?
there is one final block

Teetering.

Ricci wants to stay so
I make my excuses and leave him

My eyes hurting from all the hiding
From all the masking

All the pretending
I walk to the car

The sound of the people partying grows dim
Some relief sets in
At least it's over
What day is it I wonder?
It's still Sunday

There's still plenty of the day left for regret
I get in my car, and I drive home

Alone

Bereft
Lost
Spent

For Aiden.

You're still one of us

He says he felt abandoned
When his sister and nephews left
It's not strange like my wife said
It's true

He was abandoned
Left

While we all went out
And found a life

The oldest of 5

Still pulling on a shirt and tie
Still sitting in a chair
Still standing up to quietly sing
Still closing his eyes in prayer

Still in a crowd of faces where no one knows he's there
Still clutching the bag under his arm
Still walking next to dad
Still listening to his extended ideological rants

Still waiting for mum to place the food down
Still there at the table we used to eat round

Still in his own head

Still tormented
Still alone
Still unknown

Still a pool of darkness
Still mumbling 'yeah'
Still dreaming of being 7 years old and longing to be back there

Still brain damaged from psychosis

Still my older brother
Still unnoticed

Still one of us
Still awkwardly cared for and loved

Still here
Still near

There's still time
We're all still here

Not abandoned
You're still Loved

You're still
one of us

Based on true events

Olly and Marie

Olly and Marie were driving in a car
On a first date they hadn't got far

They pulled up at a crossroads
Ollie's glance at her was warm
His face creasing into a huge smile
That went all the way up to the corners of his mouth
Showed his teeth and flushed his cheeks
Hit his blue eyes like sun light dappling a stream and
Marie well ... she fell right in

Her eyes were steady and set
Big and brown beautiful but rarely met with anything like this
In that moment she fell the hardest she had ever fallen
On the way down all the way from her stomach she hit euphoria
Passed through fear and crashed into a giddiness

Something closely resembling happiness
She felt the back of her legs go numb
The hairs on the back of her neck stood up and she felt
Lust and longing and love swimming all together in her veins and felt the chains already forming

She allowed this to show

In the smallest way possible while she held herself still
The edges of her mouth lifted up ever so slightly
Into a tight smile bashful

And there they were
Both held in that perfect moment
At the crossroads frozen
And as he pulled away his expression changed to total panic and movements stilted and frantic

She didn't see, her face was locked on his
She didn't see the truck about to hit

Marie took the impact fully
The truck spun the car on a pulley 180
The sound of the metal smashing was sickening but it all happened in an instant
The quickening

Olly stayed gripped to the wheel
His fingers glowing white from the effort it was taking

His breath shallow and quivering his heart pounding like a jackhammer
Ears ringing
He looked to his left where Marie should be sitting
But there was just a seat

Marie was missing
As was the windshield
With blood around the edges of the cracked glass dripping

Somewhere in the midst of the collision and the spin
Marie was flung through the windscreen

Panic gripped him and he fumbled for his seatbelt
and threw the car door open

Only then his ears tuned in to the sound of the horn blaring
The truck drivers head resting on the steering wheel
The world staring
He hobbled to the side of road and found her lying

Marie lay prone
Her arms raised like a boxers covering her face
Whimpering like a wounded animal
Her face shredded with glass

Olly felt the waves of disgrace
Her eyes darting all over
Her body riding the wave of the shock

Olly tried to find some words of comfort
But he had none
He heard a car arriving and turned on his heels running
Flagged down the driver

Spread his arm to point
He still had no words.

He knew he should have gone to be with her
Held her hand but in truth it was enough for him to simply stay

When every part of him was telling him to

Run
Away

He had only met her proper that day
First date
You don't owe her nothing he heard the voice of his father say

He stayed at a distance and watched her get loaded into the ambulance
Watched the blue lights as they flashed off into the distance
He could still hear the horn blaring as the policeman approached him

He could still hear her whimpering
See her cowering

He couldn't meet the man's gaze

He still couldn't find the words to say

He noticed her blood on his shoes

And in that instant turned
and ran away.

Names have been changed to protect the innocent

'The flying fist the smile and the eye'

Pete Kelleher punched me in the eye
In the cloakroom in 1989
It wasn't exactly a haymaker, but it left me shocked and half blind with surprise
With a tiny bruise to my 10-year-olds pride

In the cloak room at the days end
Bustling excitement all nervous energy led
Someone knocked into me
I knocked into him

He whirled round to see me smiling and said
Something with actions cos' he didn't have the words to express
His spitting rage at my face
But in my defence, I'd like to say

This was how my smile was meant
One of shared camaraderie at our predicament
An elbow in the side
A wink of the eye

A raised eyebrow Roger Moore James Bond style
The bustling excitement of the home-time

 'Oh, what a carry on eh Pete??'

I guess he saw something different than what I had

in mind ...

In the blink of an eye, he reached back and let fly
His fist connecting with my eye
A flash of white and a giant Batman sign!
KERBLAM!'

I stumbled back with silvery stars in my eyes
Held my head to a chorus of disproving cries
And a few '*are you alrights?*'
But nothing too meaningful cos everyone wanted to get out of there, right?

I shook it off said I was fine
Sucked the tears in and hobbled out into the light
Back to the bustle of the tide
I tried to shake it off I really tried

I saw my mum and she knew but I wasn't bloodied or bruised
'*What's happened*' she cried?
The inflection in her voice one of fear come alive ...
The dramatic shrill cry unplugged the dam and I let fly ...

Snot trailing, eyes burning
Marching back to the scene of the crime crying and I saw Pete sitting in a car idling
I then became the shrill accuser's cry
'*It was him!*' I blubbed

And he looked on half bored
While commanding his chauffeur '*drive drive!*'

Oh dear I cringe as I think back
It all fades to black
As mum and I enter the school and as for the memory
That my friends is that

Before that fateful day in the cloakroom
I felt sorry for Pete for a long time
His grey shirt oversized
With cuffs perpetually unbuttoned and flailing by his side

He held himself awkwardly
Neither fat nor thin with a bright light on his head flashing
The weirdo kid
The one with fleas
Every class had one of him

Collected every day by a cab
Whisked back to the lab
To be dissected vivisected
Exposed to viruses with his sweat collected
Directed to wee in a cup
So it can be tested

Pete Kelleher, were you bred in a lab or in a care home
Far from the prying ten-year-olds eyes
I guess I had some kind of cautious vigilant mind
You were different
Needed some love and care

One time we were playing as a large group
Tag or it and you were 'up' it seemed unfair
You were 'up' for too long they were ganging up
So I let you tag me

A small act of kindness
From the sickly skinny boy with his hair shorn short
With a keen eye for justice but tortured by the thought

I am different from the rest
Far from the best and if anyone tries to be my friend
I'm sure that will end
So I'm sorry that my smile was plastered on my face all wonky and wrong

I'm sorry I let myself be misunderstood all along
I'm sorry you felt different too
I know not what became of you

I hope life worked itself out for you
I'm sorry for the smile and the shrill pitiful cries

I wish I could have slowed down the moment
Seen the punch before you'd thrown it
Caught the thought in your head in a net and sealed it and owned it

Or took a step back to avoid the flying fist
Or just took the hit
Or hit him back harder
Or just admit

I don't like hitting and I
Don't like being hit

Maybe it was fine
I got hit in the eye
It hurt and I tried not to cry
My mum saw my pale little face and knew
something wasn't right
I lost control and cried like a child

But that's what I was right?
At ten years old that's more than fine
I wasn't a tough kid and I'm not a tough guy

I'm a 40-year-old father of 2
With lots of pock marks on my pride
But this can be put to bed
It's time

For me and Pete
For the smile and the flying fist and the eye
And the flashing white light and the ringing in my
ears and the bruise to my ten-year-olds pride it's all
fine …

I bid it all …farewell and

goodbye.

Pity is pointless

'A bit of dignity please'

Have you ever seen an old person
Shuffling and stumbling
Encased in beige and the ruins of old age
Heavily lined
Shrivelled and sunken

Leaning on a cane
Walking with a frame
And felt the same sad refrain
Swim up from your stomach Into your chest

And beat its wings while the strings build and swell
The echo racking your bones like hell
The crescendo, pushing endorphins

Rushing like rats escaping From a burning building
Through your bloodstream overwhelming
A shameless pity that erupts with a whimper
And a titter as it enters contact with reality

And what it really is
Is a shrug rewritten and recast as a virtue in cut glass

The music swells and after all that bombast all that comes to pass is ….

'Awwwwwww'

A pitiful sound reserved only for babies and cute animals
Pity
What a pity to land so squarely and unfairly on the square marked pity

Pity without action is as meaningless as malice
To feel it bubbling up it feels like virtue, but it's actually callous

Why would you pity a long life lived?
They didn't arrive in this life withered and wizened like a tomato sundried
They have had a life and a hell of a one too

They have felt the rush of first loves
The exquisite delirious pain of heartbreak
They have looked up at that glorious painting in the Sistine Chapel and felt the pain
They have lived through history
Seen this all before

They were there and they are waiting and ready to share it all and more
And they would do to, if you only took the time to find out by offering a small semblance of dignity
Instead of sympathy

And they would be lifted up out of this vicinity
Be blessed with something approaching divinity
And the symmetry of their wizardry
Would leave you struck dumb glowing white with ideas infinity

It's here all for you to see
Right here in front of you and me
Open up our hearts to the greatness of others
And we can be similarly held aloft transcending all reality

And we could glimpse a better way to be
For you and me
And all of us
The human race

One big family
By choosing dignity
Not mawkish sympathy
A slap in the face sentimentality
That's just plain banality

So can we be better please to our aged population please
By giving them a chance to be the people they always were please
Because personalities with rich lessons and stories are waiting round every corner
And we'll all soon be

In the same spot
Clad in beige
With the ruins of age circling us
A mere stone's throw from the grave

With a few words left to share on the page before we fade
Let's start now

And hope it catches on
By the time we get to that ripe old age.

Beyond the provocative title I am trying to write something that both believers and atheists can equally like, or equally despise. I am trying to bring them together through a collective dislike of my poem. I am effectively doing god's work.

God is dead

God is dead
I killed him
I shot him in the head
I took his body
Dragged him by his heels
To an open field
And left him there

One guy was upset
'Heyyyyyy ... I liked god'
He complained
*'He helped me through
When my brother died
I got on my knees to him
Every damn night*

*And beseeched him with tears
And he gave me the strength to make it through the years
For my wife and my kids
If it wasn't for him
I'd be face down in a ditch
Or propping up the bar with my chin
I'd be nothing without him '*

Then I felt bad for killing him
Who is this guy going to pray to now?

So, I gave God mouth to mouth
And he started to choke and splutter and come round
And he pushed me off with an almighty shove
The shove of the almighty God, and at the same time, he shouted *'gettt offf me!*
'I'm not dead you fool. I'm God. You think you can kill me by shooting me in the head??
I rose from the dead!!

Shooting me in the head
Jesus Christ

I just wanted a rest
From all the prayers
And bullshit
I don't outsource this shit
I hear all of it
Every bloody word
It's a curse

As if I could ever do anything to help
I gave them free will!

You know what though

I've listened to the disembodied and detached voices of my progeny for thousands of years at this stage, and a few years ago something occurred to me, you know what occurred to me?

*The power of prayer isn't that I'm listening or even that
I exist at all it's that they think I do
It's a placebo*

I only wanted a bloody lie down ...'

So there you go
I killed God
Then I brought him
Back to life

I was never dead in the first place!

God
Not dead then

Send up a prayer

I dare you

I dare him

For my poetry pal Ally.

The artist /narcissist

Half artist
Half narcissist
A bargain basement bastard he is

Bastardising your brilliance
Beautified by your eloquence

The apathetic indifferent

Even your diss track is wrapped in sun kisses
Soundtracked by the bird song
Written across northern skies
With streaks of red, amber, and gold

I'd just call him a prick
And move on
But you leave footprints of hope even in shallow snow

You have to

Bitterness can't abide you

The alchemist of the glassy parts of the universe

You see the mountain

And paint it in lush blues

Orange hues
And vivid reds

Then climb it

The artist narcissist
Sketches the echo of his voice
Grows plump and satisfied
Falls in love with his own brush strokes
Takes what he can and dies

His head is full
His eye is small
Withered and limp
His heart a beating black hole

He'll hang himself with his words
But you'll find the truth
The bargain basement bastard

Bastardising the beautiful with his breath

He is not fit to hold your quill
He is not fit to mourn your death

As a teenager I used the superpower of invisibility to cope with the pure sensory and existential overload of high school. I always loved the swimming gala and sports day though as I got to be visible and popular even if only for a few short seconds.

400 metre champion

I never did much of anything
Bounced around like a pinball

Pushed and shoved
Pushed and shoved

I did not budge

A silhouette at school

A September shadow

Do you remember that day in April
Where the sun warmed your skin
But for a second it fell behind the curtain
And you felt cold?

No?

That was me

Then

The roar of the class as I pumped my puny arms

through the water
When I felt like a someone for a second
But the smell of chlorine lasted longer
And the next day it was over
Back to the silhouette of September

Behind my eyes
Something burned bright
But I didn't
So, I didn't

I was the 400-metre champ of 94
Stephen Wood almost pipped me, but he didn't
And I still have the certificate
Preserved perfect in plastic

I never did much of anything

But I did that

Written during Covid

Hope is all we have it's all we need

Whether you're sitting on your backside
Or fighting on the frontline
Our minimum wage heroes should be adding a few extra zeroes to their pay packets after this am I right? (Amen)
Of course I am, you can't deny it's true
But the irony is after this who's going to be the ones fitting the bill?

The millionaires protected the underclass will
And don't forget the
Doctor's nurse's social workers
Porter's posties and the carers
Teachers Bin men and the cleaners
There's always been more than 2 metres between us

But ...
It's not the time for settling political scores
Let's put a pause on fighting these culture wars
Let's leave these beached on distant shores
Arguing online has never been a worthy cause.

The earth seems to be enjoying it, we could learn a lesson from it
Shaking off the chains and really loving it
Green shoots of grass bursting through the pavement
The birds singing louder in glorious arrangement

The stillness serenity of a Sunday in springtime
Reminds me of a Travis line, *'every day I wake up and it's Sunday, whatever's in my eye won't go away' and I'm ... writing to reach you ...'*

Not trying to teach you, maybe ask a question or 2
Cos' it sure is a time to, think about what you need from yourself to make it through ...

Hope is all we have
It's all we need

Hey this is just a question, it's not about blame
I'm not saying you should do X Y or Z, there's a whole tin of alphabeti spaghetti on your plate.
Cos' once there was a person and that person looked like you
You were born into an unfair world and all those things happened to you

And I don't know much about that stuff, but I can assume you made it through
And I wonder what that says, really says about you?
That you didn't let it beat you? Take some time to write it down and see what conclusions you might come to.

And I'm not making light of anything, I know it's really hard
At first, I probably minimised cos' I didn't want to be one of those people that was terrified and alarmed

Anxious as I am, I get wistful
I do miss the old static, classic existential panic of old
Nothing focuses the mind like a national disaster, so I'm told
This is getting meandering, I'm taking in all the sights on this stumbling circuitous stray scattershot stroll, trying to find some hope to pass on to the fold
....

Hope is all we have
It's all we need

We can learn stuff from anything
Good can come from bad
Life is the longest lesson in the world
The best teacher we've ever had
But it's all about how we take it
We filter it through our lens
Jumble it round shove it around
So it makes even a little bit of sense

You knows those old cliches? About taking one day a time?
Maybe there's some truth in them, some wisdom from the divine
Cos a cliche isn't a lie, it's something that's so damn true that we've heard it so much we've become immune.
Power in the moments, small joys with each other, what are the things that have helped you through?

This may be a lightning bolt straight into our veins
A lethal dose of reality straight into our brains
Or just a sojourn
The briefest of stays
A lesson to change our ways?

Who knows
Hope is all we have

It's all we need

Sid vicious is dead and Johnny rotten sells butter.

Do you ever feel like you've been cheated?

This punk band looks really cool
With braces and jackboots
And sleeves of tattoos
Black and white posters adorning pub loos

They sure have riffs
To go with the puckered lips
Of their Photogenic lead singer
That Struts and twists

But this Fisher Price punk rock poet
Pokes fun at parliament
From the place of privilege

Private music tuition
Education
Bank rolled by middle class parents
The classist system

Isn't punk supposed to be
From the streets
Wrung from the working classes
From poverty?

No

The original punk band were manufactured

X factored

The X factor of 1976
Was a sex shop manager exploiting a bunch of
oddball misfit kids

Style over substance
Brands and business
'Do you ever feel like you've been cheated?'
Sneered the face they used
To sell t shirts with

The idea of DIY punk rock
Is as authentic as tik tok

Punk has always been about
Artifice and appearances

So, I guess this new band really are punk after all

Punk as a cynical marketing tool

A hopeful and loving plea from 2017

'Make it happen'

There's not a lot that sets us apart
Same sense of silliness same laugh
But it seems we tread an entirely different path

Same bricks but different shadows we cast
And our footsteps ring hollow as we pass
The rotting corpses of the past

Nothing comes easy
Thank god nothing ever did
I bounced around like a pinball crashing against people and places
With nothing up my sleeve no aces

Actually, I lie there was something that came easy
and that's lying and hiding

My M.O has always been to
Never ever be noticed
As anonymous as the mist on a winter's morning, try to catch it
It fades
You were certain it was there, it left a chill in your veins

I mean of course nothing good comes easy
It takes practice and I hate to hector because I know the words are blocked out
And the tone is like my fathers

And as much as I love that double denim rebel with his box fresh vulnerability, I have no wish to be Him

As much as possible I'll distance myself from him, I look at pictures and I know only my eyes are
Different from him
And that gives me hope
The window into my soul is different
I see things different
I am different.

I wanna listen.
Believe it or not I hate the sound of my own voice and don't like attention, so much to mention, share.
If only he would listen, he would know I was there

I won't go into an extended monologue just please if you can take just 3 words from me
Make it happen

Make it happen for your son
Make it happen for what you were and what you can become

Make it happen for your friends
Not the fairweather drink addled coke hole haggard trends
But your oldest friends

Make it happen for your wife
The one you don't sleep next to anymore at night
The one you pushed away instead of holding tight

Make it happen for yourself
For your health
For your heart
Your last breath for a new start

Make it happen for the blood in your veins
That one day will stop pumping and turn the page

Make it happen for your rage
The one that's crept up on you with passing age

Make it happen for your sadness
The loneliness that lives with the madness
That lives behind grinding teeth and twitching eyes

Make it happen for the boy you were
That giddy boy of mischievous lisping smiles
Make it happen for the man you can become

Make it happen for me and for everyone
Who wants to see you fly so high that you kiss and lift the Canopy of the sky

Make it happen for your fear and your anxiety
Like a prison
A cage you built to save yourself from the monotony of the passing days

Make it happen for the routines
The low hum of banality
The buzzing in your brain
The laws of the happy

Make it happen for the squandered lives lost to addiction
Your weakened body breaking down from afflictions

Make it happen for the saboteurs who have no clue what their worth
They piss it all away on drink and mirth
Know that one day you'll return to the earth
Ashes to ashes dust to dust
One go round the ride of your life for what it's worth

Make it happen for the one chance to be whatever you want
Leave a legacy a footprint a name
Make it happen for the pain
The air always thick with the threat of it taking over again

Make it happen for the fighter in you
The one who never quits
Who can screw it all up and still put himself back in the mix
Who can blow it all to bits and still face the world and not give two shits

Make it happen for the music you can make
The elegiac grace of the notes on the page
Make it Happen for every passing day closer to the grave

Make it happen for the bleak truth that sits snug in our souls
That your life is ending fast so you better be bold

Make it happen for the courage and the love you
have for your boy
The one thing that needs you
And it's up to you to keep or destroy

Make it happen for the 15 years you spent happy,
untethered from the constraints of the norms the
Forms of the oppression in our brains and our bodies,

Make it happen for the time you wasted
Feeling scared and refusing to face this
You think you'll be young forever but pretty soon
your encased in this

Emaciated frames of faceless former kids
Not prepared or ready for the weight of the world as
it really is

Make it happen for the pennies landing hollow in the
jar
Realising the chains and what there really for

Make it happen for the freedom that comes from
truly knowing where you are heading
Where you are going

Make it happen for the clock
Ticking down saying that's your lot
Make it happen for the bitterness
That really doesn't suit

The boy in the frog eyed boots and Incredible Hulk t
shirt so cute.

Make it happen for yourself above all else.

Make it happen.

My reverse to do list

A list of things I did today

2 awkward hugs
1 orange club
1 cold lasagna
1 cup of tea in a stranger's mug

1 slow walk up a hill
1 satisfying pint with a good mate
1 warm and hearty embrace
1 can of sparkling water

4 poems read out at the Colchester arts centre
1 long drive home as the A12 was closed
1 plate of dinner eaten late and cold
More than one new poetry pal made

On reflection, quite an ok day.

A beautifully boring man

My god Harry Styles is boring

My god Harry Styles is boring
Is he the new David Bowie?
No
He's got more in common with David Cameron
He may be tanned but he's got the same dead eyed pallor of the gammon

Yeah, I know I'm jealous of him
He gets to sing songs for a living
And date beautiful women
And he's adored by millions

But my god he's boring

And no amount of feather boas and green nail varnish will change that

Have you ever seen an interview of him?
I suggest you do

Although his soporific statements may send you stumbling into such a slumber
That's akin to a coma

Cos my god he's fucking boring

Yeah, I know I'm jealous
You got me

Of the high cheek bones
And the money and the adulation

And the fact he gets cast in movies
But for the love of Christ that man is dull
He can dress up as Dorothy from the Wizard of Oz all he likes

He'll still be boring when he opens his mouth
And ten tonnes of tedium spills out

Harry Styles
Boring

We are still not very good at helping those most in need

My puppy wants to die

My puppy wants to die
He told me on the sly
He's seen all the bad things on the news, and he'd rather not be alive

I said *'You're just depressed'*

He said *'yes, and who wouldn't be at the sight of this godawful mess'*

And I begin to laugh and jest, ever so slightly incredulous

*'You're a puppy!
Why are you depressed?*

It's all hugs and treats and fuss and
walks and love and love and love

And endless boundless energy
You should try being me
I ache every damn morning and this pain in my shoulder will likely be the death of me

He eyes me with wisely with those big sad eyed saucers and says

'Pain is pain

Whatever your age'

'Let me get your ball' I say

'No don't.

Stop distracting me with shiny things

Just let me be '

'I just hate seeing you this way'

My first honest statement

'It's not your fault' he says

'It's just hurt on top of hurt.'

I finally snap

'I found your goodbye letters!

Granted it was just a load of paw prints but still

…. How do you think that made me feel? (dare I make this all about me)

What happened to my happy little boy?'
(I guess I will)

He's a puppy and he's got some teeth on him but
He does not bite

*'He got overwhelmed I guess
With all the hurt and sadness '*

I let the words turn to smoke rings and disappear

'Just sit here

*And know
That life is never fully in your control*

*And when you agree to love someone
You are signing a blank contract
Making an invisible pact
With whatever is coming down that track'*

'Ok I'll try and do that'

My puppy wants to die
And I don't want him to
But I'll sit with him

And wait for this moment to pass
And remember

All things do

I saw a Facebook post that was written late at night and then hastily deleted in the morning, so I think the author realised what he'd done. Unfortunately, I'd already seen it and immortalised it forever in print.

The homeless girl

I met a homeless girl on the way home from the pub
I was red faced and giddy with booze
Tipsy
Topsy
Topple over soon probably

I'd be fine if the pavement stopped moving
My head was swimming
The streetlights were shimmering
The stars tiny pricks in the distance glimmering

Plenty of tiny pricks in the distance clamouring
If there's a damsel somewhere man, I'm stepping in
They won't win

A sucker for a damsel, I've always been

I've drunk enough booze for the courage to finally set in
I push my shoulders back and start to walk like John Wayne did
The strut that came from tiny feet in cowboy boots squashed in

But It don't last long

The pavement takes a wild lurch downwards
And my left knee gives way

Like someone flicked the pavement like a magician flicking the tablecloth
And yes, like the salt and pepper pots 'I am still standing!'

Just like the Elton John song and as I stumble along
I mumble along a couple of lyrics from the pop Don

I pass a shop doorway and see some legs and some eyes
They lock onto mine
She gives me a tight smile

She has a shopping trolley full of bags parked next to her
I sit down, get her name and we start talking

Homeless
Addicted to crack
Tut, tut I think
Fancy that

I have somehow sobered up enough to listen with empathy
I get up and think of how this powerful girl has empowered me

To be a humanitarian one day
Start a soup kitchen
Be a social worker

Petition the local MP to build a homeless shelter

Or start a 'go fund me' to get her a top-class London lawyer
Or pay for her to go to rehab
Or move her into my house
Or let her sleep in my shed?
Surely, it's better than these stone steps.

But I don't do that
Or any of those things
Instead
I write a status on FB

Saying I've met this amazing girl
And how drugs are bad, but this girl is not a criminal
The comments I get are praising me for being a nice guy
But this is not why I posted this long story alright

It's to raise awareness

Sure, I used her real name in the post
Sure, this moment of connection has now turned into a boast
And now it's the record of a good thing which somehow matters the most

Did I turn this girls plight into a fetish and make it all about me?

Am I sitting here counting the likes 1, 2, 3
Am I getting a warm fuzzy feeling inside of me

Do I feel like a better human for simply talking to somebody?

Social media is all adverts
Statements
And documented actions
A real life cannot be documented adequately in this kind of space

Those who need help are not heroes to be deified
They are just flesh and blood humans
With some slightly harder edges
From some slightly harder times

Maybe next time
I'll keep it in my head
Allow myself the time to think on it
Cos social media has turned everything into a performance

So, ask yourself
Am I doing this for me or some imagined audience
I am doing this for someone else
Or just trying to score points from this

Cos the point Is missed
In between the ads and the abs
The conspiracies
The hot takes
The protein shakes
The entrepreneurs telling you about all the money you can make

Here's my story about a girl
Homeless and alone
Click a like and move on

Forget her in an instant

I woke this morning and forgot her in an instant
But I didn't write about that on FB

Instead, I took a picture of my breakfast
And counted the likes

1, 2, 3 ...

Men will continue to kill themselves until we become more comfortable with male vulnerability.

Man flu

He arrives late to the zoom call
Full of apologies
False gaiety
Forced levity

Forced
False
Fallacy

Someone enquires after his well-being
He stutters and splutters
Caught between honesty and pride
Telling tales of symptoms but assuring everyone
he's fine

That pesky Covid booster
It's bound to happen
Up all night with a sore arm
It's fine don't be alarmed

Someone from the ether
Hiding behind their initials
Utters the phrase
'You got man flu Dave'

There are some titters, murmurs some outright guffaws! Of course, it's all forced

Keep it light
Keep it light the team manager implores

Dave frantically rubs his chin with the top of his hand
His face flushed beet red
'I don't actually get man flu, my wife does though 'he says ...

More chuckles
More plastic grins

The manager with a tone straight from the top drawer of compassion training she learnt from HR

'Oh, but you're ok though yeh?'

'Yeah, yeah. It's just this arm' Dave reassures

Dave gets lost once again
In the gallery of faces
I thought for a second, I saw his eyes glisten and sparkle slightly with tears

The conversation has moved on to more pressing matters
But I can see Dave start to crumple and his camera disappears
Replaced with a static semi stylised picture of his face from happier years

Dave doesn't have man flu
He doesn't often get ill

He rarely if ever complains

About his many aches and pains
The 2 words start to mock him
Push him around

Back and forth
He starts to break down
He mutes the meeting

Closes his eyes
His shoulders shake
His presses his fingers to his temples

He cries

He gathers himself
He looks up at the screen
Only his picture flashing on the screen

Man flu?

'Fuck you'

The inventor of the mousetrap wore that power very lightly. He was a humble man.

Pound shop Moses and the mechanical Red Sea

I pull my car up to the barrier and press the button
It is 8.53.
Look at me!
7 minutes early!

I buzz again
Waiting in earnest for the disembodied voice
The ghost from the ether
To grant me entrance

But there's only silence
I look in my rearview mirror and see
A pound shop Moses staring at the Red Sea

She unfolds herself from the front seat
She sidles
Saunters
Mozy's

Brandishing a badge tied up in a cherry red lanyard
I turn
I am a tiny head
Twisted on my neck

She says flatly with a voice coated with contempt
'They don't get in till 9'

I show her my badge and say I'm new
She holds her badge against the tiny black square

Similar in size to an After Eight Mint
The barrier opens miraculously
And she pouts her lips
Tosses her hair

The charge of power crackling in the air
Thunder and lightning bolts from the sky
She is the storm raging above Mount Sinai

That's not a work badge
That's a stone tablet in her hands
Gods Ten Commandments inscribed to man
With his big fat god finger

Blam blam ba ba blam!

I drive in
Find my space
Say 2 hail Mary's for my saviour
How can I ever repay ya?

Sometimes Love means letting go

Dear bro

Dear bro
There are some things that you should probably know
Some new
Some old

Some buried
Some left out in the cold
Some long forgotten lost souls

Remember back in September
You talked of making amends
And how you were doing so much better
In a better place
New job, girlfriend
The world had better make way!

Well, I guess that moment was like the English weather
Subject to constant change

You never did mend things
You never did apologise
We met for one drink and the scales fell from my eyes
My misplaced hope
Drenched in a rush of sentimentality and sepia hued memories

The love I'd had always returned to me
I invite you back to play music again
Back to the studio
Back to my band
The thing I'd built with my own bare hands

And dear bro
It felt good
To have you back from the dead
Cos' my dear bro I never wanted it to end
But I was so hurt It had to
But now things are different, and we can stick together like we used to

Playing guitars in the box room in greenfield
Awkwardly trying to hit the high notes
Singing 'we live in a beautiful world'
Playing FIFA on the n64
Picking 'you and me' films to watch at the cinema

And now you've got a girl who loves you and will be there for you
And everything is rosy
I know it is cos mum told me
And she wouldn't lie
She's a good Christian lady

After 6 years I'm thinking maybe just maybe ….

Dear bro
So, your back in the cell again
Back in your own self-made hell again

The devil rung the bell again
And you came running

It's sad to see the truth of what you are becoming
But I'll stick around
And I'll tell you what I need to
Try and lay some kind of path to guide you
Your crying in my kitchen telling me all you've been through

What you really want most is a hug from mum
The last time we spoke she was playing dumb
Said she didn't know anything

So, I call her and say I don't believe you and he really needs something extra from you
His mind is splintering like the hull hitting the rocks
I tell my dad to pull up his socks
And light a lantern and walk with him
Show him the way

He feeds me a line of shit
Too busy in his own head
Cultivating and curating the museum of guilt
He's got himself a brand-new exhibit to build

And dear bro
This is hard for me
To stick around
While you do this to your family
The ripple effect
It's touching everything and everyone

No one is getting away clean
Especially your own son

I kick you out of the band
You say you understand, and you will be back
Once your better and get this monkey off your back
The guilt hangs heavy
The rope goes slack

Dear bro
I guess I have to go again
I can't be party to this collusion
This illusion

We grew up on delusions
That dad called faith

But I can't survive on the fumes of lies anymore mate
There are some things that can't be prayed away

I'm ready for the truth now
You better make way

Dear bro
You'll always be dear to me

But you won't be near to me
I'll love you from a distance

At arm's length
I hope you don't fall

I won't be there to catch you
After all

Dear bro
this is the art of letting go

No

No

No.

Wrote this on a particularly gloomy Monday in January

A depressed Monday

The word depressed means when something is pressed down
A grey, wintery, drizzly, damp autumn leaf squashed underneath the worn-out tread of a moped
A lollypop lady head to toe in ultraviolet green and industrial solvent orange, shuffles past the empty
School with a Tesco shopping bag, with her shoulders sagged

It's half term
She's got no kids to usher across safely to school
In her shopping bag is stale bread
She's off to the duck pond instead

A man walks his dogs and lets them sniff every scent, staring blankly, depression is having no thoughts in your head
Blank and bare as a mountain of Viennetta squares

Eyes get itchy from seeing too much
They get weary, they yearn for bed

Depression is wanting everything to end
Depression is every sound putting your teeth on edge

It's the upside down inside out crisp packet in the hedge

It's lonely here he said
To himself
In his head

The cars glide softly by like a hot knife through butter
Nothing stops or stutters
Life keeps moving
24 hours a day

7 days a week
There will always be footfall on the streets
Mobile phones pinging
Microwave meals ready to eat

Fork at the ready to kill the plastic sheet
Watch it spin around
And wait for the sound
That tells you, you need to get it out

Life gets smaller and smaller
Like looking through a telescope through the wrong end
Sit on the sofa and watch your tv
Don't smile
Or laugh because you don't do that unless you're in company

If a lonely man laughs at Del Boy falling through the bar does anyone hear it?

No

And if he dies will anyone see it?

Don't waste time arguing online. Create something instead.

Jimmy is not a meme

I see a post on Facebook
A poem with a picture
A bedraggled and bloodshot eyed somebody
By the name of Jimmy

The writer paints a picture of a romantic figure
Moving hither and thither
Like an autumn leaf on its way to winter
Like a twig on a river

Free as a bird
Dancing in the autumn leaves while we chumps prepare for winter
Tuned in to a frequency that we just can't understand man
Yeah, it's called schizophrenia

A transmission from a barren wasteland
But this guy's mystical
Wearing that *'crazy smile'*
Subsisting on fag butts, cheap cider and rock and roll

Rock and fucking roll?
Are you kidding me

The writer gets close and thinks he can hear the

music too
'What a guy Jimmy is
What a life to live
Free from all this social media and woke bullshit

They are pulling down our statues
Tearing down our land
The Queen couldn't take it anymore and that's why she died man
Jimmy, you keep doing you my good man'

You are romanticising a mentally Ill old man
Fetishising an open wound in a bloody hand
Deifying the goddammed
Man oh man

There is nothing romantic about schizophrenia or psychosis
What on earth made you want to post this?
All the little Englanders underneath it getting all teary eyed with emotion from this
Daily mail readers

Tory voters
Can't connect the dots
From their thoughts and fears
To the smiling face on the billboard over here

From the glossy campaign video
The Union Jack rippling in glorious sun dappled slow mo
To Jimmy's face and his fate
Why are you getting all gooey eyed mate?

His fate was sealed while you were banging on about snowflakes
If you care so much about Jimmy
Take it to the ballet box
Or give some of your haves to the have nots

Or give some of your time
Or think for one fucking second before you post this shit online

But I thank you
For giving me something to respond to
I am moving away from defining myself by what I am in opposition to

And learning what it is I want to stand for
And that is against people like you.

For Marilyn

20 years too late

She died in 2024
But In reality
It was long before

In the year 2001
Her husband
Put her beloved house
Up for sale

He wanted to retire
To rural France
This was always the plan
Now here was his chance

They'd not talked about it
Because they never did
With them two
There was nothing too profound
That could go unsaid

They both broke the sound barrier
In that they never made any
For the eternity of their matrimony
They passed by like
Shadows on a sundial

Neither knew one another
They just created each other

In the gaps
Where loved should have lived

She had her life
Her bingo nights
Her friends
And a job that was alright

He had his ferrets, frogs and newts
His fishing, his trivial pursuits

But when the house sold
She left her life
And followed her husband
Like a dutiful wife

A house with a swimming pool
Up a winding cement road
Not a neighbour for miles
A lost and lonely abode

The space between them both
Now filled with sadness
And cigarette smoke

The boredom boiled
Into a broth
That turned
Into a clot

That seeped into her synapses
Found her left hand brain
And collapsed it

The words turned to slurry
In her mouth
As her face drooped
Like a melted cheese welly

She stumbled
Stricken by 3 strokes
Smote
Smoked

Broke
And choked

She stuck it out for a while
Trapped in the ruins
The wreckage of her body

Before one day
She found the words
She needed to say

'Let's go home, eh?'

Her husband
Smiled
His famous toothy grin

And she turned to butter

'You've gotta be joking'
He muttered

He then said

With all too indecent haste

'You can go if you like'

In those 6 words
Lived a lifetime of shrugs
And her father's absent
Kisses and hugs

'You don't mind?' She managed.

'No'

She forced a tight smile
And turned away

She came home
On a one-way flight
Alone

And stayed in her
Dead mother's home

Surrounded by school photos
Of her kids from long ago

With long forgotten haircuts
And smiles subtle and small

Before moving into
The waiting room

Where she stayed

For 20 years

Words
To her were
Merely
Vases for dead flowers
She lived with none

She left with none

She was sent on her way
In an empty carriage
With a eulogy
Licked onto a postage stamp
20 years too late

A rare call to arms

An amnesty

Is anyone else sick of politics?
Is anyone else sick to the back and front and false teeth
Of the festering swamp that belches and bubbles underneath

Sick of the culture wars
Which the right blame on the left and the left do likewise
Who's right? Well it depends on your tribe
And what piece of state propaganda you choose to imbibe

Can I make a suggestion?
Can we please have some kind of amnesty
Can we give up our weapons just for a week
Can we put a pause on fighting these culture wars
Can we do something truly unique

Of all the people I've met and liked and disliked
It's never been because of them being left or right
We've boiled everyone down to their least interesting human aspect
And used it as rubric, a measuring stick, to judge others and extinguish our own shortcomings with

But not all lefties are nice and not all Tories are scum

We are better than these simplistic notions that's
point number 1

Imagine if we just put all this shit aside just for a
week
Imagine what we could achieve

Turning off all our devices
Laying down our weapons

Could very well be
The biggest act of civil disobedience in history

Hitting them where it hurts
in the algorithm

They wouldn't know what to sell us
Sex, holidays, hobbies, politics, sports
Stag doo destinations, all our little predilections, the
single biggest act of disruption, saying no to
pointless scrolling into oblivion. yeh? Yeah??

A great poet once wrote
Let's press pause on fighting these culture wars
Let's leave them beached on distant shores
Arguing online has never been a worthy cause

It's easy for you to say
I hear you cry
You're a Straight male, Cis white
Some of us wear our culture and identity and it
brings a spotlight
We can't just put it aside

I know
I'm self-aware enough to know that
After all, you know I wrote this bit
and that bit before

I'm not talking about cessation I'm talking about a ceasefire
Even the forces in the trenches put aside their mandated ire
And they were in an actual war
Bombs bayonets bullets
And boys
Baked in blood
Christmas day they put aside the flood

I think things have become too complex
We need more ambiguity
We need more nuance
With the Simplicity

Can we agree it's not good to hurt people freely
Whether in word or in deed

Can we agree there's some things which transcend politics
Can we agree that the young have verve, gusto, and enthusiasm but also immaturity and a lack of
Understanding of how things generally go

Can we agree we shouldn't discount someone just cos they are old

Can we agree that shit rolls down hill

And inevitably it's a Woman who ends up eating it though

Can we agree that sexism likely exists in the marrow of our bones

Can we agree calling masculinity toxic might not be such a good way to go
Can we agree that pornography is likely warping the minds of everyone who sees it and it will always be so

Can we agree that woman can take control of their own bodies and they should do so
Can we agree that to be trans is surely the toughest of roads and they need love, kindness, compassion and understanding, no?

Can we agree it's not right to steal someone's livelihood and shame them
Can we agree that a person is bigger than the boxes that we choose to contain them

Can we agree that everyone is probably trying their best
Can we agree that the nuances of most complex arguments cannot be adequately expressed within the confines of 280 characters or less

Can we agree that a comedian's job is to be funny
Can we agree that there is such a thing as having too much money

Can we agree that lefties are sometimes insufferably smug

Can we agree that right wingers care more about a foetus, than they do about children in a boat on the channel capsizing and dying while trying to reach us

Washing up lifeless on a beach, what the hell?
Surely this kid means more than a bundle of cells

Can we agree that things are better now than they used to be
Can we agree that it's a good idea to have a good secure nuclear family

Can we agree that a family doesn't have to have a mum and dad for it to be good or bad
Can we agree that an amnesty would be good for a week for all humanity

Can we agree that most cultures were built upon the blood and backs of people of colour and that Is just a fact!

Can we agree the media lives and breathes on the worst kind of news and tragedies
Can we please agree to turn off all social media for a week

Can we turn off all media please

Let the green shoots of our best fruits start bursting through the roof
Let our lost youth have a day off from this never-ending anxiety loop

Let all the noise of Elon musk's ego go unheard
Let the airbrushed hyper filtered influencers of
Instagram silently polish their turds

Let Facebook get buried in an avalanche of unread
posts and words

And let tik Tok
Fuck right off

Let's breathe in some air

And make some eye contact and get back in touch
with our best selves and start to care
This amnesty mate

Let's try it what the hell
I'm starting now who's with me

Who's with me??

For Luke. My knight in shining armour

Kurt Cobain's myth making nearly gets me punched square in the kisser

In a dilapidated old boozer
With cobwebs for curtains
And smoke rings for coasters

As inviting as an abandoned submarine
Where the barnacles have taken over

A punter was piqued by my choice of attire
My Nirvana t shirt making contact with his ire
He slouched over like a piss artist
Shaking hands with a fire

His words slid out in a slurry
'Kurt would have hated that shirt '

My ever-present sense of self preservation
Kicked in
So, I decided to agree with him

'You're probably right '

Because it was quicker and simpler to agree

'Do not throw pearls before swine' God once told me

This guy had fallen hook line and stinker
For Kurt Cobain's knack of self-mythology

His eulogising
Soliloquising
While his star was rising and rising
He was trying to live the life
And do his own bio writing

The reluctant rockstar trope
Is money for old rope

Slayer of big hair corporate cock rock
Purveyor of perfectly pitched pop music
Drenched in feedback

The soft Pisces boy
Cut from angels' hair and baby's breath
Strung out on heroin cos of the fame
Until his untimely death

But he signed for a major label
Made sure he got pretty much all the royalties
And always dreamed of being a famous rock star
He wanted his songs played on repeat on MTV
He wanted to go far

And as for my t shirt

I reckon he probably couldn't give
A Flying V shaped shit
What I use to cover my upper body with

RIP
Kurt Cobain
None of us ever knew you

Childhood longing never leaves us

A hug from the moon

The boy waited for the house to grow still
For the hustle and bustle to quieten
For the murmuring to cease
For the moon to untether itself and be released

He popped the window
Inched out onto the ledge
Threw his body onto the flat roof
Stones crunched and scattered
As he tip toed to the edge
Folded his legs crossed and sat

The moon was big and bright and bathed him with a pale light

'Come down please' he pleaded
'You're all I have left. Hold me tight in your silvery embrace and take all these aches away, to the place you go in the day. Or take me with you please, to the horizons end and we'll stay locked in each other's arms forever and we'll travel the whole world over together '

It was the same refrain, every night the same
But the moon stayed slung low in its place and never budged an inch or moved its light from his face
He promised himself he would still keep coming
Up to the roof every night running
He would never stop

Wanting
Wishing and waiting

For the hug from the moon
That was never coming

Not an excuse for nihilism, but a way to ground even the most anxious of hearts

Life is absurd, people are ridiculous, and nothing matters

How could you walk out into the world
into this theatre of the absurd
And take it seriously

Life is hysterical
Stupid
Full of dopey
Hokey
Half arsed
Rules

We still have Kings and Queens like we live in a
Disney cartoon
We doff our caps
Pay our tax
Line the streets
Like peasants begging for scraps

Bread and circuses on repeat
We worship what we pay for
The Queens face on our currency
I reckon they close those palace gates and just laugh and laugh
They can't believe they are getting away with this shit

Prince Charles once had a servant who squeezed out his toothpaste every morning
I wonder if he even knows how to wipe his own....?

Now
He is the King
Because his mum
Who let's face it
Seemed alright
Died

Schools love to teach us all about empire
How to be good little patriots
Queen
Country
The Colonies
Not murder
Mayhem
Slavery
Subjugation
Those crushed under the weight of this nation

The school's walls emblazoned with motivational quotes
'life isn't about avoiding the storm it's about learning how to dance in the rain'

While they force neurodivergent pegs into neurotypical holes
And dig shallow graves for all the anxious souls
Teach us about empire and how to be good little citizens

Our politicians crow about morality
While selling weapons to Israel
And the Saudis
Who cares about a few dead Palestinians and Yemenis?

I'm amazed they can walk a straight line
With their crumbling spines
Their values are chem trails in the skylines
An exhalation of air
A puff of smoke
A magic trick
A dead rabbit pulled from a hat

We deify babies and children
And demonise teenagers
We hate the elderly
And have put on a pedestal
That most self-centred of decades
Our 20s

The young have got their looks sure
But nothing more
No money, no job prospects, no children, and no houses to live in

No planet to live on
No future

Climate change activists
Desperate to change this
Capitalist narrative
Spray paint stone henge and disrupt the cricket

'No!
For the love of god!
Not stone henge! Is nothing sacred???

Whisper it
But denial
Is kind of important
We need it
If we didn't have it
We'd all lay down in the street like in that Radiohead video

Sometimes the denial switch
Malfunctions
We call this 'depression'
The floodgates open
All we've been holding back

We need to get this good little worker ant
Back in the conga line
We all need to do our bit for Queen and colony

If you can't flick back that denial switch through talking
We use medication
Get those dopamine receptors firing

The old have homes but can't get rid of their adult kids
They can't move out coz they can't afford it
'Renting is just dead money'
isn't all money dead when it's spent?

We hate everything going up
But property is fine
'What am I supposed to do with this investment?'
I don't know
Maybe
Live in it?

Capitalism has infected every area of our lives

'Hey'
'I am just waiting for my folks to die'
I'm not gonna lie'

Speaking of capitalism
America rebranded this successfully
As the American dream
And sold it to the world

Read some John Pilger (God rest his soul) Bill Blum and even Media Lens
It will all make sense
Hollywood convinced us all that America are the good guys
The world's policeman
Clumsy
But concerned with the law
Well meaning

Empires care about power
And they'll crush any dissenting voice like an ant under their star-spangled jackboot

Here's a bleak prediction

Donald Trump is going to be the president of the US
for the second time
No amount of felonies
Controversies
Scandals
or pussy grabbing can stop him

Some view him as the ultimate anti-establishment
politician
A man who stands up to the system
And not someone who is an integral part of it

But that's not the funniest bit
There are some
Their brains seasoned by the salt and vinegar of Fox
News and the Bible Belt TV evangelicals who actually
believe that Trump has been chosen by God himself

But that's not the hysterical bit
There is another layer to this wedding cake of idiocy
who believe he is some sort of cosmic crusader
involved in an epic battle of good and evil with a
secret cabal of child murdering blood sucking
paedophiles
That operates out of a Pizza Hut

The world is absurd
Nothing matters
Go forth
Be happy

For tomorrow
We die

So at least for today

Smile

You're alive

I don't know what this is about

My kid could paint that

The man spent his days
Stealing birds from trees
Stuffing them into glass jars
Labelling them in alphabetical order

Dreamer
High achiever
Anxious non attender
Up his own arse

He saw the light from their eyes
Grow dim over time
He wondered why

He took photographs of pylons
Lampposts and stop signs
Exhibited them alongside his birds
He sold the pylons for millions
The birds he couldn't even give away

Fame is fickle, I'd rather be a nobody forever

Big cheese

Once he was a big cheese
Now, a nobody
A faded 70s rockstar
Keeping his hair long and daubing it with tar
The same colour of the leather of his pants and jacket

He squeaks when he walks
They call him tight arse racket
Coz he nurses a half all night
And doesn't shut the fuck up

Regaling bored barmaids
With tales from a bygone age
Of groupies and band mates
And the roar of the crowd from the stage
Cautionary vapour trails of booze and cocaine
'It was mad mate, it was insane'
But I'm not proud of it he says
Somehow with a straight face

Finding his old bands songs on the jukie and sticking it on ten times in a row
As the bar empties, he's left swaying
As he's told to piss off home

He stumbles on sticky tarmac
A walking talking preening pouting panic attack

He pours himself in through his front door
A slow and steady pour
He is nose to floor
Dust and dirt and nothing more

He steels himself to scream
Contorts his face
With one last glorious flourish
A final encore
Plectrum in hand

His heart stopped beating
And that was that

Curating your social media as a twentysomething is its own full-time job. Gotta be informed but not smug.

#Trainwanker

Fast food
Instant friends
Coffee to go
Lie in on the weekends

Pronouns
Rainbow
Ukrainian flag
All in the bio

Palestine is trickier though
My boss might see it
And let me go
I need this job
It's not just me
I gotta think of my family

Swipe left
Swipe right
Wipe once, twice
3 times

No time for breakfast
Chug down some Huel
It's got all the greens I need
Rocket fuel

Follow all the hashtags
Share it all to my story
Micro plastics? tick
I know the meaning of real politik

Quick guardian article on fracking
Don't really understand it
But I'm sharing it
It's happening

Stephen fry is worried about the BBC
Something to do with the licence fee
I don't really watch tv
I think I might have ADHD

Do a quick online test to see
It says you are highly likely
I don't read the disclaimer
I text my mum and complain to her

She replies *'oh ok'* which I smile at
Go to type back
Then she says
'I think we're all a bit autistic'

Bloody boomers

Generation rent
Be thrifty
Save that 1.50
By the end of the year
You'll have enough for a deposit

'They didn't have avocado toast in my day
They didn't have Netflix subscriptions and Apple Pay
If I wanted something I had to work for it
This generation want something for nothing'

I share the article and call them c***s, change it to dicks instead
Just in case my parents see it, start charging me rent

Take a selfie on the train
#trainwanker

Put it on my story

Not all goodbyes should be sudden

Who will get custody of all the good times?

Who will get custody of all the good times?
That one is yours
This one is mine

I'll have watching you round the corner from the front door
Coming back from the job you hated
In that trouser suit that you wore

Rounding the corner with a ready smile
Ring still fresh on your finger

I'll have
Me sitting
By the bath
Where the bump sat above the water
Talking to our daughter
Asking
Is she awake or asleep?

I'll have
Painting the nursery yellow
Getting giddy over buggy's, changing tables, nappies, cotton wool, muslin squares, miniature vests, Baby grows, socks and assembling a cot bed

I'll have

Bringing her home
Broken sleep
Minutes, days, hours on repeat

I'll have us watching shit TV
Coz that's what we need
Grand designs
Come dine with me

I'll have
Our first holiday
In Yarmouth

In a wood chalet
With an
Outdoor pool

I'll have
You under the glowing white of incandescent sunlight
The smell of new life

I'll have the red hair on their head
And their name on my breath

I'll have that last look on the landing
When your blue eyes shone
Like summer blue afternoons in June

When you said
'I still love you; you know?'

And that's all I needed

I'll have that
I'll keep it safe

I won't forget

The only thing worse than change is things staying the same

Ash

You live in our old house, the one on Greenfield. It's all boarded up now. The colour of ash.
Half burned down ten years ago; the roof is missing. It's covered with a green tarp that makes a rippling sound in the wind.
Plywood is hammered across the bottom windows, and it's tattooed with mindless graffiti. Tar black shapes that look like letters. A broken filling in a row of pearly white teeth.

You have used a crowbar to lever apart the back door and this is how you get in and out.
Mums brand new kitchen, dusty, dimly lit and damp.
We used to sit round the table and drink red wine and make jokes about people looking like objects.
Brian is a picnic bench etc.
In the living room you have a small mattress and a kerosene lamp and stove.

You want me to come here so we can play guitars and laugh like when this house had an upstairs.
When there was carpet, and the smell of bacon would drift through the house on a Sunday morning.
When you escaped through the downstairs window to go to the fair when you were 13, when we'd play FIFA, and I gave you your first beer. When Aiden's mind was just starting to break but you couldn't see

it on his face. When Hannah was just a little girl who sold lemonade in the park and really wanted a dog. When all the worlds sadness was held in the pages of a dusty old text. When everything made sense.

You want me to sit and warm myself by this lit cigarette while we reminisce. But I can't get the smell of smoke out of my nose, I can't stop staring at your broken teeth, I can't sit here in the dark of a burnt-out house and make believe.

Outside the sun is shining, my kids are waiting.
I wish more than anything to see you again in the sunlight.

The fridge magnet philosophy never saved anybody

Dear person in front of me

I am standing behind someone
In a queue
On their jumper there is a message that says

'Dear person behind me'

'The world is better with you in it, from the person in front of you'

Something inside of me
Starts to beam
I feel seen

I tap him on the shoulder to tell him
He looks annoyed, takes out his headphones, keeps his phone in his hand
Doesn't fully look round

Does not smile

I want to tell him how depressed I've been feeling
How I wake up every day with an anvil in my head and an elephant on my chest

How I just can't seem to sleep but all I want to do is rest
But I can see he doesn't want to talk

So I say

'Sorry I thought you were someone else '

I stare at his message on the back of his jumper
I want to write the truth on it in a big fat magic marker

I know why people kill themselves
Because real human connection cannot be monetised or commercialised
And it takes more than 35 quid to save a life

It takes more than the time it takes to shop on Etsy for something under the category of 'wellbeing knitwear'
It takes more than the time it takes to cut and paste

The Samaritans number onto your social media page

I just want everyone to know that when someone's struggling
They have never had their life saved

By a Facebook post

A t shirt
Or a hashtag

I just want everyone to know that someone is always listening

Yeah, google

So it can sell you anti-suicide merchandise

The rest of us are just lost in the noise
Lost in the cacophony
Of footfall online

'Please listen to my new single

I've just found a dead cat

Sorry guys I've gotta rant

I just saw Will Smith murder a tramp'

Dear person behind me

I can hear you screaming

But I don't have time to listen

This mostly all happened in 2006

Written, directed by, and starring me

I went to work in a psychiatric hospital
Thinking it would be like a movie
Where I would meet someone
And him and I would go on a journey

We'd start like a classic odd couple
Jousting and bickering
That eventually grew to grudging respect
And we'd break out under cover of darkness

Go on a trip to the seaside
I'd learn something profound about myself
While helping someone else

And there'd be a montage scene
Where we'd tip toe on a high wall
And eat ice cream

And try on different sized hats in a department store
And get chased out by the security guard
But head straight back in for more

There'd be tacit acknowledgment that this needed to end
So I'd drop him back and we'd part as friends
And I'd realise something trite like
We are all the same underneath different types of rubble

And his smile would be the last thing the audience would see
Before the credits roll

And it would say
Written / directed by and starring me

But it wasn't like that at all

There was a sex offender
Soft slipper shuffling in his dressing gown

An overweight girl in her 20s
Arms lashed with self-harm scars
Being followed by blank eyed robotic staff

The air popped and crackled as a man stomped around with his top off
Itching for a fight
Like this was a kebab shop on a Friday night

A tall man
6 foot 2
Bashfully showed me his drawings
Slightly screwed up bits of paper
Scrawled with stick figures

Later he'd smash up the telephone
Because they'd ordered in
And he wanted a Chinese

The smokers room

Foggier than a Kate bush video
Sat in the corner like a rotten tooth
With ghosts sunken eyed in the window

A procession of half bored
Half arsed staff

*'Keeping everyone on an even keel
Everyone calm'*
Intoned a pragmatic
Bespectacled
Medic

There was a staff nurse named Gus
With a squashed bouncer's nose
And a pugilist stance

He told me
'Get ready, we're gonna take Mr bare chest down'

I panicked and told him
I didn't know how

He frowned in disappointment
Disbelief
And barely disguised hurt

I realised then this was not for me

I leafed through a hospital magazine
While Mr bare chest was taken down
In a high-pitched clamour of howls

I could still feel Gus's frown

I unbuckled my keys

And let myself out

This poem does not contain paid advertising

Subway was invented by a man who hated people who loved sandwiches

You'd be forgiven for thinking that the proprietor
and principle provider and promulgator of the best
Damn sandwiches this side of the Mississippi
Would be a big fan of sandwiches himself but no
He hates sandwiches
And hates anyone who loves sandwiches too

Oh it seems tantalising from the outside
Sun kissed airbrushed hyper filtered
Hearty Italian loaves
Bursting with ham, Turkey, cheese with a coke and cookie to go

But when you get inside
You'll make more decisions
Against the clock in seconds
More than you've likely ever made
Or will ever make again

First
Choose between these 25 types of bread
Don't take too long will you
There's a queue of people behind you
Chop Chop

Next choose a filling from 37 available combinations

Right, salads next, that should be easy
Salad is just lettuce, cucumber, tomato, right?
Wrong! There's gherkins
Pickles
Diced onions
Red cabbage
Olives!

Then they hit you with something simple
Do you want it toasted?
Do I?
Who knows?

My brain is cauterised
I've never made this many decisions in my life

Mr Subway
Just a little FYI
If your favourite food is sandwiches
You're probably a go with the flow kind of guy

Not a ten-year planner
Or a hedge fund manager
Venture capitalist
Buying this sandwich was like being on the shop floor of Wall Street

Buy low
Sell high
Get me a tuna salad on rye

I just want to sit in my pants and eat subways till I die

But I won't do that
This amount of hoops to jump through just isn't worth it

So instead I'll sit in my garden chair at home
Eat wafer thin value ham straight from the packet by the bucket load

And charge my glass with it
And raise a toast

To Mr Subway
Torturing sandwich lovers since 1965

Hope the bastards still alive

So I can punch square him in the eye

The cheeky chappie shtick does get old after a while

An arm in cast, a brain in a jar, a liver in vinegar

You have grown more childish
But you think it's charming, boyish
You flirt with the nurse
While she puts your arm in cast

She asks if you've been drinking
'That's outrageous' you laugh
As a can of 1£ cider falls out
Of your back pocket while you fall apart

You are a stand-up comedian on stage
In a sparkly jacket

'Look at my brain in a jar'
'Here's my liver preserved in vinegar'
'I'm on the list for a kidney transplant'
'I'm yellower than Bart Simpsons bare arse'

You are 13 again
Popular in school
Loved by us all

Everything in front of you

Social media has baked all our brains

Man tries to discuss the enlightenment with a sausage dog

Man walks two tiny chocolate covered bourbon biscuit sized sausage dogs
They are both under his feet
Barking at everything from leaves falling lazily from trees
To crisp packets loose on the breeze
And at my dogs and me

'Stop it' The man says

'You know better than that Emmet'

'Remember all those Sam Harris videos we've watched together on man not having free will?'

The dog continues to bark

I turn and say to him
Don't worry mate

I know the dogs weren't your idea
You got them in a fleeting moment of romantic attachment to your partner
Or you're a pushover

You remind me of Saturday night fever by the bee gees

But instead the main character has low self esteem

'I can tell by the way you use your walk
You're a mummy's boy with no time to talk'

I think
You think that you are somehow getting this dog walking thing all wrong
You've been suckered by the plinky plonk Toy Story piano reels of cute little dogs

And when you're out on a walk you think that everyone is judging you
So you tell your dog off out loud so I can hear it
But

Just cool it

Your dog needs a walk you walk it
The dog feels like barking at a leaf he barks at it
Take your time
Let them sniff a patch of grass for an hour
It doesn't make you a failure

For them this is like going to a wine tasting
All the different brands and types and bouquets of piss
'Oh yea this reminds me of a good Bordeaux from 1700s'

You can't get walking the dog wrong
You're doing a good job

You're fine

But he rushed past
Chiding Emmett
Saying
'You have humiliated me for the last time'

'Hang in there Emmett'

I yell

Poor dog

Some honesty in the midst of all the nonsense

Good boy

Good boy
Wants a pat
On the head

To be told he's good
Wants a hug from every woman
But also secretly wants to sleep with them

Good boy
Sucks the exhaust pipe
At both ends
Early morning
Late evenings
And weekends

Spends hours
In reveries
Of imagined conversations
Frames his own decisions
As discussions
Playing the pronoun game in his head

'He's a good lad, a good friend and dad'

Good boy
Will bury his head
In a book
On geopolitics

Knows the difference between
Naomi's Klein and Woolf

Tells his therapist
He'll be buying
Bukowski
Just to see her eyes
Flood subtly

He has browsed that bookshop many times
Felt the weight of that book
Held it to his chest
Flicked through it
And always tucked it back with the rest

Good boy
Tosses exquisite
Hand crafted
Coins
Into the abyss

He is the perfectly placed
Hymnal book
Lined up
Arranged
In empty church pews

Good boy
Wants
Yearns
Paws
At the door

For something
On the tip
Of his tongue
A dream
Of more
Evaporating

Like a dead dandelion
In the spring breeze
Disappearing
With bird song

Summer skin
Pale shins
White socks
Pulled tight

Oversized white
Basketball shoes
Hair grown out
Unruly curls

Open fields
Blue skies
Swaying trees
Like drunks
Unsteady on their feet

The silence
Punctured
By bombs falling in the distance
And blossom

In his nostrils
Brittle boy
Anaemic
On anti-biotics

Hospital bed
Rhythmic beat
Heart monitor
Doctors

Nurses
Clipboards
White boards
Strip lights
Blackcurrant cordial
With too much water

Good boy

For the one that got away

My blue haired Clementine

Driving the same roads
Swerving the same potholes
A different girls voice this time
Fills the silence

You came back
With a yearning

My blue haired Clementine

I attached weights to your body and pushed it down
Watched you drown

I find your picture
Unblock your number
But it's been 7 years
You no longer remember

When I last saw you
You looked down
I thought we might
Have shared a small smile
Even a frown

One day I'll figure it out
In real time
Not 7 years down the line
Wizened, wrinkled, hand knitted and pickled

I say
I don't understand romantic love
Never did get it
Feel sick and uncertain In it

The waltzer of the heart

I say it enough
Enough that it starts to take root
Like a lone man in a church pew
Admiring the ornate architecture
While smoothing out the feathers of a dead bird

What I wouldn't give to talk to you
But your 7 years ago
And we no longer exist

I made a ruin of it
Made it sordid
Believed the lies

Saw with a lifetime
of Old Testament eyes
Made love askew

Once
We had a piece of bone
We used to pass to each other
A little piece of me to take home

'Let's get matching Puzzle piece tattoos'
Yes, it makes me cringe too
But you don't care when you're in love do you?

'You're the missing piece of me' is a big red flag apparently
I don't know if I'm in love or unwell mentally

I was not sober
Or clear eyed
But I've never loved another
With the same hunger

I've never loved another with the same hunger

I forgot you
I painted you red
I made a decision to hate you instead
It was easier than admitting it

That I loved you then

And all of it meant something

Meant more than anything before and since then

Back then
You were everything

The past is the present

Mr Velcro can't let it go

Mr Velcro can't let it go
Don't even bother asking
He just can't you know
All his girlfriends, one-night stands, brief dalliances, it's all still in his hands

They should have slipped through his fingers years ago
There's Sonia Smith
The girl he fancied when
He was 6 years old

His first girlfriend
Who drew half her eyebrows on
Who he loved with a fierceness that shook him
She's there too
42 years old
She looks sad
Her red haired now laced with cobweb grey

They used to pass notes to each other
When they had the energy

Rachael the Australian
Big brown eyed
Fond of Elvis and bongs
And footie and horses
Who didn't eat red meat

Hums Guns and Roses tunes on repeat
Attached to his legs are his brother
And his dad
His dad wouldn't stop talking
That's why he is gagged

He's still chatting away
Muffling along
Weirdly he still looks
Quite happy

His brother is on his leg
With tangy apple-soaked breath
Telling Knock Knock jokes
Laughing himself to death

Mr Velcro man
Sometimes feel bad
And they reminisce
About the old days
The first girls they kissed

When Velcro didn't exist
When the world was all Empire magazine
And cinema trips

When love meant doing things
Treating his siblings as kids
Before life came
And stole them away from him

When his body was lean
Lithe and light

And he would glide
Through life

In a slow-motion daydream
Of a human being in flight

Before gravity
Before Velcro

Before the weight of the world

Where do you put a lifetime of hurt?

A pragmatic decision to hate you

I've made a decision
I've decided to despise you
Because I've got too much anger
The kind that slowly poisons you

Right now I'm living in a hoarder's paradise
Surrounded by tower blocks
Of yellowed tabloids
Polaroids
Snapshots of a life

An art piece
Welcome to all the fragile messy
parts of me

I need a place for all my ire
And I've made a pragmatic decision
To throw you on the pyre
Play pin the fury
On the donkey

If I don't decide to hate you
It will eat me up inside
Turn into a blood clot or a cancer
A growth
A lump
A hump
An arthritic stony spur

I've made a pragmatic decision
It's not in any way personal
It's healthy
To find a rightful place for something

I kept an apple on my desk for ten years
Till it had grown yellow like the stacks of tabloids
Sure there were flies
But there was comfort in getting something right

I'd never resort to violence
I don't want to hurt you, you see
Unless you try and hurt me
But that would never happen
Because you don't know me

And I don't know you
Your just a face on a billboard
On a magazine rack
If we passed in the street

You wouldn't look back
Because you hate someone else
And it's better that way

Put it somewhere

Like a pet project
A hobby

Hunt elk
Kill zombies
Hate the Tories

And sleep soundly
The blissful sleep of the happy

The man who knows what nothing means

And where all his anger is kept

My dad should get royalties from this book

Bernie. The musical.

There is Japanese knotweed
In my garden
My dad hears of the problem
And sends a barbershop quartet
To sing me songs by Alanis Morrisette

I did a sponsored busk 14 years ago
He still sends me busking videos
All our correspondence
On a way radio

I send poems by telegram
They come back undelivered
He offers to manage my band
But he wouldn't know how to do that

This one man play
Performed
Off Broadway
Since 1979
Has grown dull

I know all the songs
The dance moves
The one liners
The encores

I just don't know the ending

When the show finally finishes
Will I miss it?
Will I wish I'd have taken more time to see it?

I very much look forward
To beating myself up about it
That will be a worthy and fitting tribute

Will I find myself one day
Humming the same songs
Making the same moves
Stuck in the same groove

Sending clips of My Chemical Romance
To my 40-year-old daughter
Watch them go unopened
And wonder why

Send flowers to her workplace
Imagine the embarrassed look on her face
Feel all good memories fade
Start my own 1 man play

Even on our worst days, we are better than him.

If God was good and kind

If God was good and kind
He'd have made 50 Adam and Eves
So they could have had friends and parties

He wouldn't have used them as chess pieces

He'd Just occasionally check in on them
His creation, his new species

Give them some kind of guidance on morality
Not just a partner, a job, and a list of rules to obey

Actually if God was good and kind and smart
He'd have noticed

His spirit son gone wayward
Grown distant

He'd have booked in some time
With him

Seeing as time meant nothing to him
He sat outside the finite
He could have done that

He could have saved him before he made himself the devil

If God was good and kind and smart and decent
He would not want one bended knee

No rosary
He'd say stop with the building of the expensive churches

I'm not impressed with stained glass windows
Built off the backs of the poorest
Your Kings and Queens I have no interest in saving

If God was good and kind and just and decent and loving

He would not want one cruel act done in his name
He'd make that plain

He'd send miracles
Not plagues

10 feats of wonder
And
Not murder
He sure don't half love a good murder

If God was good and kind and just and decent and full of love
He'd not wrap everything in ambiguity
Mystery
Medieval bloodlust and misery

Prayer would be reversed

His thoughts beamed into ours

Transmitting hope straight into our brains

If God was good and kind and just

He'd be less like him and more like us

For every child in care

You can't be properly parented by a bureaucracy

You can't be properly parented by a bureaucracy
The local Tesco can't bring up a child
We don't let Primark raise children

The shop is set up to sell discount sweat shop manufactured clothes
Stock checkers can't breast feed
Store assistants don't know what to do with a colicky baby

The security guard can't read me a bedtime story
The lady on the till doesn't love me
Minimum wage pays for exactly that

John Lewis sells beds so at least I have a nice warm place to sleep in
And many different types of mirrors to do my make up in
But the shop shuts at 5.30 and all the lights go out
I wander quietly in the dimly lit dark bumping into things

The security guard won't play *would you rather* with me

I would rather I have a family

The instore cameras follow me as I leave via the exit door
The cameras in the street pick up my trail
I am last seen heading for the bridge

McDonald's gets the late-night call that I am standing on the edge saying I'll jump

They keep asking if I want fries with that

I am happiest on my own

The room

Close the door
I'll line up the cars
How I want

Lie on my side
Feel the carpet
Tickle my cheek

The room has a slow heartbeat
Green eyes smile softly

There is only ever me

In this room
I don't have to worry
About being a good boy

Or if my mum will have red eyes today
Or if she'll tell dad to pack his bags

The eyes of my star wars figures
Are painted a warm brown

They only get angry if I want them to
I whisper their words in an American accent

I can't hear anything
The room is so still

I am at play
I am making things
That will evaporate

My door is closed
I am happy

The well wasn't always dry

Dry wells

You were born in the dry wells
With only dust to play with

Clay to kneed together
Make bread with

The smell of the sea
Would arrive on a stiff breeze

And shake the trees
Silently

A red kite caught your eye
In summer Blue sky

You only knew
Dusk and dull light

Anything else
Made you tired

You traced a heart around it
With a fingertip

By moonlight
You threw out a wish

Your eyes cut into diamonds

And cast adrift

Cigarette ash loose
On the lips

'This

will be

the life you missed'

I decided to write a poem about my hometown. The glorious Witham.

Under the bridge downtown in Witham with Anthony Kiedis and Alicia keys

Some people imaginatively call Witham

'Shittam'

But I think it's alright

It's got a river
It's got a Lidl
It's got a Polski sklep

If Anthony Kiedis from the Chilli Peppers lived in Witham he'd be singing about it all the time

He'd walk bare chested into town
Past Tommy Tuckers, the best damn chippy in the land

Past the Bric a brac
Cut glass crystals
Any old tat shop
Oddly named

'Past caring'

Which I think is a clever way of saying second hand
Whereas I read it as

'We gave up giving a shit years ago'

He'd pass the Wetherspoons and the charity shop
The first of many
He'd wander in

And pick up ten VHS cassettes
A floral print dress
And a signed autobiography of the people's Princess

He'd carry his newfound purchases
And start to hum a tune

*'Sometimes I feel like... there's such a thing as too many charity shops
Sometimes I feel like .. every man here has a window cleaning round
Is the city I live in ... not a city but a town
Lonely as I am .. oh look .... a Prezzo'*

He'd walk through the old precinct
The ugly duckling of the 2
Past Iceland's, Clinton cards
Farm foods

Peek into the window of a shop that sells mobility scooters
Ironic
Considering
Here
No one is going anywhere

Cross at the pedestrian crossing

Where The White Hart pub
Has been sitting
For 200 years or more

On sawdust coloured
History books
Of this town
From yore

Anthony keeps singing

'It's hard to believe that ... anyone would live here
It's hard to believe .. one place can have this many barbershops
At least I have her love ... although she barely seems to like herself
Lonely as I am ... in that cafe you can get an Olly Murs breakfast'

The second precinct is slightly
Gentrified
With a Costa and a Tesco
But it also has The Works and a Poundland so it's still a work in progress you know?

Stop for a moment
Smell the air
And you can taste the scent of the
Industrial machines

The steel toe boots on
The floors of the factories
At the edge of town

By the rush of the A12

'I don't know ever wanna feel ... like those poor drunk guys in the park
Take me to the place I love ... to the river walk
I don't ever wanna feel ... as invisible as I did at school
Take me to the place I love ... to my friends, my family my kids'

Anthony has made it
To the river brain
And he's bumped into Alicia Keys on the way

She won't stop banging on about New York

Concrete jungle
Where dreams are made of!

Alicia give it a rest

Me and Anthony leave

We start to sing together

Under the bridge downtown ...
Is where I lost my swimming trunks
So we went into the river to find them
We stayed in there for hours
In the filth of the river
With branches and bracken
Shopping trolleys
Shopping bags

Trying to build a dam
Me, Paul, and Tel at 10 years old

The closest I've got to heroin
Is being in the brown of that river
Surrounded by old spoons and TB

Under the bridge downtown in Witham
Anthony and me

And briefly

Alicia keys

Things fall apart

The Cold War kiss

The cold war kiss
Dryer than a frostbitten Fingertip

Too numb
To clumsily unbutton

The hand knit
straight jacket

One night
All the words spilled out

And you didn't know
What to do

With all the mess

The tale of me getting murdered by a load of beardy singer songwriters

Frank Turner has a lot to answer for

Sitting minding my own business
In what looks like a hospital waiting room
Another fellow traveller sidles over

With a question
Unsteady on his lips
A query at his fingertips

*How did you come to be
Holed up here in purgatory?
Halfway between heaven and hell?*

Well my friend I've got a story to tell

It started with a simple plea
At an open mic
Off Victoria street

I said

Can we all
All of us agree
To have some sort of amnesty
On shouty singer songwriters please

On beardy bellowing in a regional British brogue
Sped up yelled up roaring covers of Kylie Minogue

Hacking at a battered old acoustic guitar
Patched up with patchworks of stickers of 2000s alt rock stars

And talking too much between songs and peppering every other lyric
With clusters of F bombs

I'll tell you
Something

Frank Turner has a lot to answer for

But it's not his fault
They've all forgotten his more tender moments
The plaintive piano of Jet lag
The waltzing guitar of Cleopatra in Brooklyn
The subtle heartfelt plea in the simplicity of Be more kind

Not every song
Is a non-serviam
Not every lyric is shouted
Like the Queen is dead

So can we please call time on this right now?
And tonight if you see one of these guys start to shout
Say

Hey man
You've got a microphone
There's no need to yell

I'm right here
Sing me a lullaby
Something sweet
Not frank Turner knock offs on repeat

Woahhhhh!

I appear to have angered them
Now I'm being chased down Colchester high street
By an army of shouty singer songwriters
With sharpened guitars like pitch forks

It was just a joke I yell
A wry take on the music
That guys make
On the sheer gall
It must take

To think
That all you need to do for a guy
Is shout over open chords
And it will magically open all the doors
You'll be showered with applause and piss poor music awards

If a woman tried this
She'd be laughed out of every venue in town
This is a feminist call to arms
Wrapped up in a court jesters' gown

Aaaaaaaagghhhhhhhhh!!

Anyway that's why I'm here
That was my last act on this earth mate

Yep
Your right
Not all heroes wear capes

Not all heroes wear capes

I bought this guys book as a present for my sister and ive never felt so ashamed

The diary of a psycho CEO

Welcome to
The diary of a psycho CEO
A glossy podcast
That you probably know
Interviewing famous people like Seth Rogan and Louis Theroux

The host seems genial
Although when pressed about his success
He never says he was luckier than the rest
There's obviously something indefinable
Indescribable that makes him the best

Scrape beneath the glossy surface
And conviviality
And you'll see
The super charged venture capitalist psychopathy

Ready yourself
Steady yourself
Disembowel and

Disembody yourself
From all the vestiges of your humanity
Human reality

And doff your cap

Deferentially
To our over lords
The Kings and Queens
Of all things monetary

Here comes one of the Kings
One of the Dracula's of business

Asked about work life balance

He said you can't have it
If you wanna build something that's gonna last
Like Enron, Pan am and the Fyre festival
You gotta put the time in

Here's another one

'I love firing folks on Fridays'
I love ruining lives on Fridays
I love wrecking peoples' weekends'

And our genial and affable host just laughs

The corporate Vulture
Cackled at her cruelty

Do you want to know the crime?
That would cause the firing.

Negativity

Those mood killer's man
Those energy vampires

Banging on about
Regular Office hours
Bathroom breaks
Sick pay and the living wage

Pensions
Equality
Sexual harassment
All while taking part in dress down Fridays

'*I can't carry those people*' she said
As if she's Christ carrying the cross

And not just someone who employs people
You know like, a boss.

If you want the rainbow
You gotta put up with the rain

If you want the pyramid scheme
You gotta put up with the pain

Jeff Bezos should take a leaf out of her book and fire his folks on a Friday for being negative about pissing in water bottles.

I wonder how many depressed workers got fired on Fridays and killed themselves on the weekend?

That's next time

On the diary of a psycho CEO.

Therapy is paying people to listen to us

Smudge

I have a smudge of black on me
It may be permanent

My therapist tells me
Don't worry
It's not

Good

It's been there a really long time though
Longer than I've known him

He just nods at this
I wonder what he writes on that pad

I get home
I've been watching true crime documentaries
Like the rest of the world

Since Covid
The rise in fear fuelled content has rocketed
I should have invested
Instead all I have is these damn bottles of hand sanitiser

I have bought an infra-red light
And a rudimentary kit
To dust for prints

Therapy taught me the power of reframing
So I'm not alone
Single
And the wrong side of 30

I am a gumshoe
From a film noir
A loner
In a black and white film from the 50s

I dust the smudge on me
Use the tape in the pack
To find a print
But alas no match

Because a database is something I don't have
It didn't come with the testing kit

I'd have to upgrade to get it
And I can't afford it

I ask my therapist
'Who do you think these fingerprints belong to?'

He looks at me
Momentarily
With honesty
Before switching back to the
Soft face of therapy

'Who do you think they belong to?'

'You know what? Sometimes it would be nice just to be

told something new about myself
I live every minute of every day In my blind spots
There's only so much I can know about me
How about you tell me what you think for once? '

'That's not my job' he says with a smile that hits me as smug

'How convenient' I say

'Maybe the fingerprints are from all men who have held me down? And there's no match because there's just hundreds upon hundreds of them on top of each other, and you're just the latest in the long line of emotionally unavailable guys that I'm sitting across from wanting something you can't give, and what makes it even worse is that I'm paying you for the fuckin privilege'

He shifts uncomfortably in his chair
Looks at his watch

We are nowhere near finishing
But times up I guess

I shake my head and get up

At the door I turn back
He looks sad
His eyes are big like a puppies

I smile and say

'I'm not sorry'

We can be lifted, liffffffftttteeed

Kill me now

I have a small bag of dog shit in my pocket
This chair is giving me piles
And they have just started playing the Lighthouse Family

Kill me now

It's the only sensible option at this stage

Hit them where it hurts

The algorithm does not care
About any politics
It likes to know what you like
So it can target you with shit to buy

It is indifference personified
It cares nothing for left or right
The world burns
While the algorithm churns

The revolution will begin
When everyone starts writing
Fuck you Zuckerberg under
Every Facebook post

Fuck you Musk
Under every tweet

Fuck you Bezos
in every Amazon review

Fuck you Bartlett
Under every podcast

Fuck you

A true story

AA but for people addicted to business

In a dusty old community centre
Where the echoes rise from your feet
Up your legs, judder your spine
And pinball off the high ceiling

A man puts out chairs in a circle
A short man in a suit
Grey beard and hair
His familiar face clenched like a closed fist

An orifice
Of avarice
A master of the black arts
Of business

It's Alan Sugar from The Apprentice

This is the first of its kind
For addicts of a certain type
Enabled, aided, and abetted
By the capitalist menace

The room soon fills up
Here's Elon Musk wearing a jet pack
All the dragons from the den
Stephen Bartlett
The CEO from Pret A Manger
Richard Branson

Jeff Bezos
Mark Zuckerberg
Mary Barra
Rosalind brewer
Safra Catz

They mill about the tea and coffee
Toss a tea bag into a Styrofoam cup
Fill it up
Shovel in instant coffee
Swirl it around

Turns out
Shit coffee and Tea
And the hall of a community centre
In Hackney
Is a real leveller

No booming voices
Bravado
Bonhomie
Incandescent under industrial strip lights
There's nowhere to hide
They are reduced to mumbling teens
Kicking their heels
Elbows pocket deep

How did they get here?
The invitation was explicit
They had to dress down
And get public transport

Stephen Bartlett secretly hoped it was

The Secret Millionaire
A chance to show his good and benevolent side
That capitalism can be both cruel and nice
Philanthropic and kind
But he soon realised

It was Sugar who set it all up

It was time to confront themselves
And work the steps
They were all hopeless addicts
The biggest and most damaging on the planet
Their rampant rampaging rapacious
Rhetoric had ravaged and raped
It was time for much needed change

Steeped in denial
Centuries old
Cutthroat pirates
Silver and gold

Pilfering and plundering
Pillaging and conquering

Now

Pontificating in Podcasting
Masquerading as Dragons
Tormenting ten gung-ho
Exuberant young men for sport

And It runs deep
All the way to

1600 Pennsylvania Avenue

Alan sugar started first
With no teleprompter
No joke writing
His opening monologue
Was frankly poor

My name is Alan Sugar, and I am an addict

The silence hung heavy
Punctured by occasional coughs

Bezos broke the silence first
'Seriously Alan what are we doing here?'

Elon then felt emboldened to chime in

'Yes Alan, I'm working 25 hours a day on this new rocket that could revolutionise space travel ...'

They all started to clamour
A cacophony of noise
Falling over each like a litter
Of puppies trying to get to their mum's teat

A gun shot rang out

Silence

Sugar was standing holding an admittedly quite small handgun into the air

'I've got your attention now have I. This is pathetic, to see you squabbling like children'

'It is over gentleman. And gentle ladies .. we have come to the end'

'The end of what?' Elon began

The end of the line
The end of the lie

The end of the end of the end

Capitalism is dead

The world is a cow
And we have milked it
To death

It's dead
We need to reinvent the wheel

We need to work the steps
We need to make amends

We need to stop blowing endless smoke up each other's arses

'Am I being punked?' Bartlett the schoolboy giggled

'No you're not being punked'

'It's us who have been doing the punking

Sonny Jim'

Without warning
They all rushed him
And so ended the first intervention of its kind
AA for those addicted to business
Spreadsheets
Corporate elites
Tax loopholes
Offshore accounts
Dow Jones
What goes up
Must never come down
The pound
Deutschmarks
Dollar signs
Lit up in red eyes

When Alan Sugar finally understood the meaning of the words

'Your fired'

Depression is the truth peeking out

Calling in sick to my boss

I can't come to work today
As I've broken my brain
I think they call this going insane

I feel ok

But my brain is in pieces on the floor
Cogs, springs, deadlines, meetings, calendar requests, tasks, admin, it's all there with blood and brain

There is a whistling I can hear
Wind unencumbered across vast open plain
Dust and tumbleweed
Broken city signs
Dirt brown
Grit and oil

I sit and stare at the sky
Watch birds in flight
My brain is now broken
But I feel alive

I won't be at work today

But tomorrow
I should be fine

While there's sand in the hourglass, there's still time.

Depressed with the potential for cabaret and violence

His swagger is sunken
Head down
Greasy palm over shaved head
Depressed
With the potential for violence

I remember him
One of the lads
Hooting
And braying
Charging in the school corridors

Smoking on the way home
Peacock strutting
Squaring up to his best mate
Headlocks instead of hugs

Bundles instead of love

His dad kissed him only with fists
Spilt milk and split lips
Good thing he was blessed
With a boxer's lightness

His mind would wander in class
Loose daydreams
The crackle of his dads

Records from the past
He'd slide in
With a Stetson
Flick it off his head and into his hand

Swish
Slide and sashay
Two stepping away

His reverie interrupted by a mate
Kicking the chair legs away

He fell backwards suddenly
Back into reality

The class erupted into
Laughter

He erupted into violence
Kissing the mate he loved
With his fists

Teacher clawed them apart
And shouted him out

Now he's 38
Soft shoe shuffling
In his slippers
On a sodden Sunday
At 7 for cigarettes

Swaggering
With his head down
Depressed

With the potential for cabaret and violence

He catches the shop worker's eye
Calls her darlin
Asks how she's doing

It's her first day
on minimum wage
She's paid by the hour
Not by the word

So she smiles tight
At the floor
While she bags up
His loaf of bread, Tea bags and more

He looks at her face anyway
Says a hearty goodbye
And when's he left
Turns the air blue
Under his breath

When he gets home
He knows what he'll find
Dad
Dead in his chair

He saw him as he came down
The stairs
And just left him there

He called his name
Ambled over

Inspected his face
Sniffed

Yep
Definitely dead
He said out loud

He switched on the kettle
But they were out of milk and teabags
He reached into his dead dad's pocket for some loose change

On his way He found himself
Unexpectedly whistling
A cheery showtune
But stopped

Coughed in his hand
Crossed himself
And spied a familiar face
Walking his dogs

A kid from school
Not a mate

He was still there on the way out
Letting his dogs sniff tuffs of grass
And take turns pissing

He bowled over
Tried to ignore the look
That fell
And lingered on his

Scuffed and bloody knuckles

'Leon, right?'
He offered up
'From school?'

The man with the dog
Who is me
The one telling this story smiled
And looked down at his dogs

My body slightly turned

*'My dad's dead
Just found him this morning'*

*'I'm not upset
There's not any part of me
That's sad
I've always hated that man'*

Ok
I say

'Could you come and see?'

To my great shock I agree

He picks up the pace and the bonhomie
The banter
'I remember you was a real geek at school weren't ya, proper swotty twat'

'I remember you being a dick' I said

'Yeah fair point'

Inside the house the man barrelled in
*'See
Look nothing'*

*'Is he dead?
Could you
You know, check?*

I took his pulse
Felt his cold wrist
This most fearsome man
Had indeed ceased to exist

Yeah he's passed
You should probably call 999
And maybe close his eyes

'No I like it better this way'

'It's fucking party time'
He said unwrapping
The plastic from
Some discount champagne

He came back with glasses

*'A toast
To the meanest bastard*

Who ever lived
Who only ever kissed me with fists'

'Whose love for himself
Outlasted his kids
And I outlasted him
I beat him'

'Do you like cabaret?' he said
And popped on a showtune

He took an umbrella
And did his best Fred Astaire
I knew it was time to get out of there

He didn't see me leave
But I saw him through the window
Head up
Shoulders back
Two stepping
Pirouetting

In front of his dads
Cold cadaver
Like
Abracadabra
The caged bird is free

The depressed man with the potential for violence, cabaret, and joy

About the author

Leon the poet is an Essex based poet, musician and podcaster. He writes personal, political and provocative poems while also occasionally writing about sandwiches.
He was raised in a high control religious group and often writes about god and belief.

TEN POETS
VOLUME ONE

MARTIN APPLEBY
DAWN VINCENT
JAMES DOMESTIC
AMY WRAGG
LEON THE POET
MARY FUCKING POPPINS
RICCI READ
RICKY FROST
TONKABELL
JACKIE MONTAGUE

Ten Poets (Volume One)
by Martin Appleby, Dawn Vincent, James Domestic, Amy Wragg, Leon The Poet, Mary Fucking Poppins, Ricci Read, Ricky Frost, Tonkabell, Jackie Montague.

The first in a series of books showcasing poets of all stripes and intended to act as a primer to check out their other work and/or book them to perform in your city, town, or village.

Poetry is arguably in (another) period of renaissance right now – everyone and their dog is a poet; just check out Instagram or TikTok – but there's plenty of really terrible poetry around, as there always has been. We don't want that stuff; we want the diamonds that sparkle in the dirt, those that are using poetry to connect with audiences, to say something about the human condition, to make people think, reflect, and maybe even laugh like drains (poetry on some level is entertainment, and only an inveterate snob would say otherwise).

For some of the poets that feature in this collection, this is their first published work. For others, these poems sit alongside their other books, contributions to literary magazines etc. It doesn't matter; they're all here in one place and demanding your attention, so dive in and give them some!

Available at www.earthislandbooks.com

E.D. Evans books available from EARTH ISLAND BOOKS

E.D. Evans is a lifelong poet. Having spent time in both London and New York during Punk's original heyday in the late '70s and early '80s, Evans has always comfortably floated between those two worlds. She became deeply entrenched in New York's East Village art scene that was so pervasive in the 1980s/90s, spending years performing spoken word poetry at venues such as The Nuyorican Poets Café, Brownies, and The Knitting Factory. Her Instagram handle, @originalpunkster11 says it all.

"I've always liked to tell dark stories that rhyme, so hopefully my words translate into the ethos and audience for which it is intended. What a lot of young Punks today may not realize is that even back in the day, Punk was always about acceptance and inclusion. We were what we were—basically a bunch of creative misfits looking for our tribe, with a great soundtrack to boot. And when we found each other, it was a glorious thing."

Evans currently features her spoken word on social media platforms, and is collaborating with an array of visual artists and musicians to bring her poetry to life. She lives in the Sonoran Desert with parrots, a blind cat, lots of backyard lizards, and a madly talented multi-instrumentalist.

"...And to all our spokespeople who have passed, Rest in Punk. You influenced generations to come, and I, for one, will always be grateful."

Available at www.earthislandbooks.com

Andrea Janov books available from **E|EARTH ISLAND BOOKS**

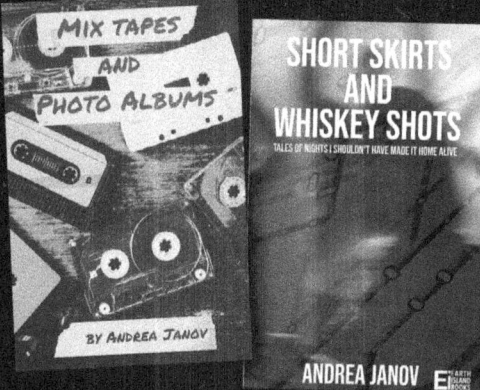

Andrea is a mess of contradictions, fan of parallel structure, and nostalgic pack rat who writes poetry about punk rock kids and takes photos of forgotten places. She believes in the beauty of the ordinary, the power of the vernacular, and the history of the abandoned. Through her work, she strives to prove that poetry can be dirty, gritty, and accessible by revealing the art in what we see, say, do, ignore, and forget every day.

Raised by rock and roll parents, she learned the importance of going to concerts and ignoring the "no trespassing" signs in her childhood. She spent her adolescence in a small town punk rock scene where she moshed, fell in love, and produced a few cut-and-paste zines, before escaping to New York City and causing a ruckus in Alphabet City. After meeting her husband in one of those Chelsea bars she has settled in Pittsburgh, is at the whim of a feisty terrier, works in tech, and still prefers Jameson neat.

After paying a few universities way too much tuition, they granted her several degrees in creative writing. When her education was complete, she started garnering some publishing credits, including a sold out run of her first book, 'Mix Tapes and Photo Albums: Memories from a small town scene'.
'Short Skirts and Whiskey Shots' picks up from where 'Mix tapes...' left off.

She is uncomfortable talking about herself, even in third person.
www.andreajanov.com

Available at www.earthislandbooks.com

James Domestic books available at **EARTH ISLAND BOOKS**

Domesticated Vol. 1, 2 and 3 available at www.earthislandbooks.com

Sam Marsh books available from **EARTH ISLAND BOOKS**

WISDOM OF THE PUNK BUDDHA

www.earthislandbooks.com

AVAILABLE FROM **Earth Island Books**

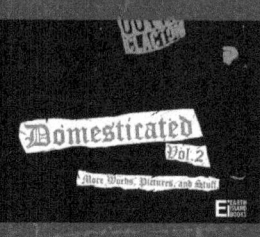

www.earthislandbooks.com

www.ingramcontent.com/pod-product-compliance
Ingram Content Group UK Ltd.
Pitfield, Milton Keynes, MK11 3LW, UK
UKHW051524050125
453039UK00009B/70

9 781916 864467